Individuals
& Societies

MYP *by Concept*

1

Individuals
& Societies

Paul Grace

Series editor: Paul Morris

Author's acknowledgements and dedication

This book is dedicated in loving memory of my mother, Angela Grace.

I'd like to thank So-Shan Au, Megan Price and Paul Morris for all their help and support with this project. Thanks also to Matt Burdett and Shirla Sum for their feedback on selected chapters.

Although every effort has been made to ensure that website addresses are correct at time of going to press, Hodder Education cannot be held responsible for the content of any website mentioned in this book. It is sometimes possible to find a relocated web page by typing in the address of the home page for a website in the URL window of your browser.

Hachette UK's policy is to use papers that are natural, renewable and recyclable products and made from wood grown in well-managed forests and other controlled sources. The logging and manufacturing processes are expected to conform to the environmental regulations of the country of origin.

Orders: please contact Bookpoint Ltd, 130 Milton Park, Abingdon, Oxon OX14 4SB. Telephone: (44) 01235 827720. Fax: (44) 01235 400454. Lines are open from 9.00–5.00, Monday to Saturday, with a 24 hour message answering service. You can also order through our website www.hoddereducation.com

© Paul Grace 2016
Published by Hodder Education
An Hachette UK Company
Carmelite House, 50 Victoria Embankment, London EC4Y 0DZ

Impression number   8
Year   2020

Cover photo © Rawpixel Ltd/Thinkstock/iStockphoto/GettyImages
Illustrations by DC Graphic Design Limited and Oxford Designers & Illustrators
Typeset in Frutiger LT STD 45 Light 11/15pt by DC Graphic Design Limited, Hextable, Kent
Printed in Italy

A catalogue record for this title is available from the British Library

ISBN 9781471879364

Contents

How to use this book

Welcome to Hodder Education's *MYP by Concept* series! Each chapter is designed to lead you through an inquiry into the concepts of individuals and societies, and how they interact in real-life global contexts.

The *Statement of Inquiry* provides the framework for this inquiry, and the *Inquiry questions* then lead us through the exploration as they are developed through each chapter.

KEY WORDS

Key words are included to give you access to vocabulary for the topic. **Glossary** terms are highlighted and, where applicable, search terms are given to encourage independent learning and research skills.

As you explore, activities suggest ways to learn through *action*.

Each chapter is framed with a *Key concept* and a *Related concept* and is set in a *Global context*.

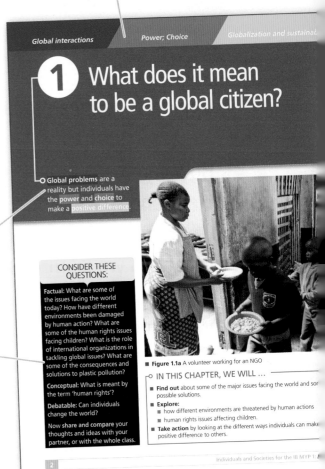

Global interactions   Power; Choice   Globalization and sustainab...

① What does it mean to be a global citizen?

Global problems are a reality but individuals have the power and choice to make a positive difference.

CONSIDER THESE QUESTIONS:

Factual: What are some of the issues facing the world today? How have different environments been damaged by human action? What are some of the human rights issues facing children? What is the role of international organizations in tackling global issues? What are some of the consequences and solutions to plastic pollution?

Conceptual: What is meant by the term 'human rights'?

Debatable: Can individuals change the world?

Now share and compare your thoughts and ideas with your partner, or with the whole class.

■ **Figure 1.1a** A volunteer working for an NGO

○ IN THIS CHAPTER, WE WILL …

■ **Find out** about some of the major issues facing the world and so... possible solutions.
■ **Explore:**
  ■ how different environments are threatened by human actions
  ■ human rights issues affecting children
■ **Take action** by looking at the different ways individuals can make... positive difference to others.

Individuals and Societies for the IB MYP 1:...

2

ATL

Activities are designed to develop your *Approaches to Learning* (ATL) skills.

Hint

In some of the Activities, we provide Hints to help you work on the assignment. This also introduces you to the new Hint feature in the e-assessment.

ℹ Information boxes are included to give more detail and explanation.

◆ Assessment opportunities in this chapter:

Some activities are *formative* as they allow you to practise certain parts of the MYP Individuals and societies *Assessment Objectives*. Other activities can be used by you or your teachers to assess your achievement against all parts of an assessment objective.

Key *Approaches to Learning* skills for MYP Individuals and societies are highlighted whenever we encounter them.

EXTENSION

Extension activities allow you to explore a topic further.

Finally, at the end of the chapter you are asked to reflect back on what you have learned with our *Reflection table*, maybe to think of new questions brought to light by your learning.

Use this table to reflect on your own learning in this chapter.					
Questions we asked	Answers we found	Any further questions now?			
Factual					
Conceptual					
Debatable					
Approaches to learning you used in this chapter:	Description – what new skills did you learn?	How well did you master the skills?			
		Novice	Learner	Practitioner	Expert
Learner profile attribute(s)	Reflect on the importance of the attribute for your learning in this chapter.				

■ Figure 1.1b David Beckham is a UNICEF Goodwill Ambassador

■ Figure 1.1c A medical NGO

● We will reflect on this learner profile attribute …

Caring – we will consider the different ways that people can make a positive difference to others and the planet.

These Approaches to Learning (ATL) skills will be useful …

Creative-thinking skills
Critical-thinking skills
Communication skills
Information literacy skills

Assessment opportunities in this chapter:

Criterion A: Knowing and understanding
Criterion B: Investigating
Criterion C: Communicating
Criterion D: Thinking critically

What does it mean to be a global citizen?

KEY WORDS

deforestation   recycling
human rights   sustainability
pollution

THINK–PAIR–SHARE

Look at the pictures (Figure 1.1a and b) on these pages.

With a partner, think about whether individuals can change the world. Can anyone change the world? In what ways can people change the world?

Share your thoughts with the class.

We have incorporated Visible Thinking – ideas, framework, protocol and thinking routines – from Project Zero at the Harvard Graduate School of Education into many of our activities.

You are prompted to consider your conceptual understanding in a variety of activities throughout each chapter.

! Take action

While the book provides *opportunities* for action and plenty of content to enrich the conceptual relationships, you must be an active part of this process. Guidance is given to help you with your own research, including how to carry out research, guidance on forming your own research question, as well as linking and developing your study of language acquisition to the global issues in our twenty-first-century world.

▼ Links to:

Like any other subject, individuals and societies is just one part of our bigger picture of the world. Links to other subjects are discussed.

● We will reflect on this learner profile attribute …

Each chapter has an *IB learner profile* attribute as its theme, and you are encouraged to reflect on these too.

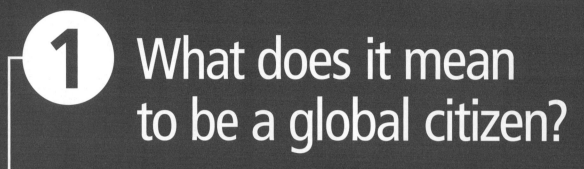

1 What does it mean to be a global citizen?

○ **Global problems** are a reality but individuals have the **power** and **choice** to make a **positive difference**.

CONSIDER THESE QUESTIONS:

Factual: What are some of the issues facing the world today? How have different environments been damaged by human action? What are some of the human rights issues facing children? What is the role of international organizations in tackling global issues? What are some of the consequences and solutions to plastic pollution?

Conceptual: What is meant by the term 'human rights'?

Debatable: Can individuals change the world?

Now **share and compare** your thoughts and ideas with your partner, or with the whole class.

■ **Figure 1.1a** A volunteer working for an NGO

○ IN THIS CHAPTER, WE WILL ...

■ **Find out** about some of the major issues facing the world and some of the possible solutions.
■ **Explore:**
　■ how different environments are threatened by human actions
　■ human rights issues affecting children.
■ **Take action** by looking at the different ways individuals can make a positive difference to others.

■ **Figure 1.1b** David Beckham is a UNICEF Goodwill Ambassador

■ **Figure 1.1c** A medical NGO

● We will reflect on this learner profile attribute …

Caring – we will consider the different ways that people can make a positive difference to others and the planet.

■ These Approaches to Learning (ATL) skills will be useful …

■ Creative-thinking skills
■ Critical-thinking skills
■ Communication skills
■ Information literacy skills

◆ Assessment opportunities in this chapter:

◆ **Criterion A:** Knowing and understanding
◆ **Criterion B:** Investigating
◆ **Criterion C:** Communicating
◆ **Criterion D:** Thinking critically

KEY WORDS

deforestation	recycling
human rights	sustainability
pollution	

THINK–PAIR–SHARE

Look at the pictures (Figure 1.1a and b) on these pages.

With a partner, think about whether individuals can change the world. Can anyone change the world? In what ways can people change the world?

Share your thoughts with the class.

HUMAN ACHIEVEMENT

Planet Earth is sometimes referred to as the lucky planet, given its ability to support complex life. Earth has just the right mix of gases for a breathable atmosphere – it is not too hot and not too cold, and there is an abundance of water. Humans have inhabited the planet for thousands of years and gradually the world has become more and more interconnected. If we consider the differences between the lifestyles of prehistoric people with our twenty-first-century lives we can see the considerable extent of these changes.

These changes have come as a result of a range of discoveries and scientific and technological breakthroughs. The interconnected world can be seen in the complex trading relationships around the world; often the items we use in daily life have travelled far to reach us. The progress of human societies can be seen in many of the cities of the world, with numerous examples of artistic, architectural and scientific achievement.

Despite these considerable achievements, there are major issues facing the world at present. In this chapter we will identify some of these issues and explore the different ways that individuals can take action and help bring about positive change.

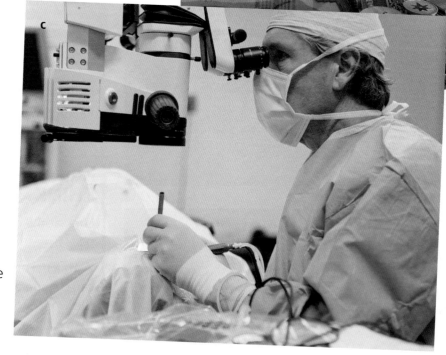

■ **Figure 1.2** Examples of human achievement

d

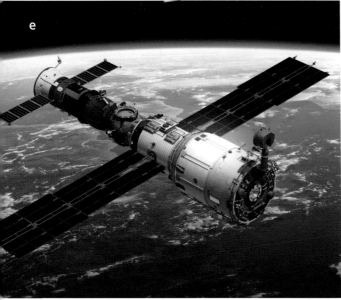

e

▼ Links to: Sciences

What is Earth's atmosphere made of? How is it different from other planets in the solar system?

ACTIVITY: Human achievement

▪ ATL

Creative-thinking skills – Apply existing knowledge to generate new ideas, products or processes

1 Look at the pictures (Figure 1.2a–e). For each picture **explain** how it can be described as an example of human achievement.
2 In pairs, **list** other human achievements from your own knowledge. You can think of examples from the past as well as the present.
3 Visit a news website and try to find an article about human achievement. This could be about a scientific breakthrough, an artistic creation or a story of heroism. Write a description of the article and **explain** why it is an example of human achievement.
4 The key concept for this chapter is global interactions. How do you think the different examples of human achievement discussed would affect global interactions?

What are some of the issues facing the world today?

ⓘ Human rights issues can often involve prejudice and discrimination.

Prejudice – Dislike or hatred towards someone based on unfair opinions, for example, racism, sexism

Discrimination – Treating someone differently, usually in a negative manner based on unfair opinions; for example, racist laws in a country

THE ENVIRONMENT – Environmental issues are a major global problem and we will examine two case studies in this chapter. Environmental issues relate to anything that is damaging or threatening to both natural and human environments. Examples of environmental damage include pollution, the depletion of natural resources and waste disposal. There are many people in the world who are committed to improving the environment and there are a variety of ways that people can make a difference.

POLITICAL REPRESENTATION – This refers to the different ways that people are governed. Many people in the world live under repressive governments where their human rights may be threatened. In these areas people often do not have the ability to choose who represents them in government.

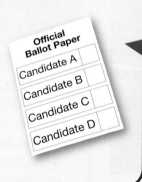
Official Ballot Paper
Candidate A
Candidate B
Candidate C
Candidate D

What are some of the issues facing the world today?

TERRORISM – Terrorism is a global issue with a variety of causes. It usually involves violence against people in the name of a particular cause. This violence nearly always leads to a lot of suffering.

DAILY NEWS
Terrorist attack

■ **Figure 1.3** Issues facing the world today

HUMAN RIGHTS – People do not enjoy the same rights globally. There are many parts of the world where different groups in society do not experience equality and, worse, may experience **prejudice** and **discrimination**. Human rights issues can also include abuses by a government to its people, such as torture. A major organization that is committed to campaigning for greater human rights is the United Nations.

WARS – Wars have shaped and continue to shape human life in a negative way. Wars nearly always involve a severe loss of life and they have many causes and consequences. Efforts to promote peacemaking can improve this global issue.

RESOURCES – Resources refer to the amount of goods that people or countries have access to. These resources could refer to food, water, medicines or schools. Issues associated with access to resources and development will be explored in Chapter 6.

HEALTH – Proportionally, very few people in the world have access to high-quality health care. There are many parts of the world where several thousands of people share access to a single doctor. Health can be seen to be a global issue owing to these inequalities. In addition, there are parts of the world where health issues can become considerably worse during times of war, natural disasters, drought or famine conditions.

ACTIVITY: What are some of the issues facing the world today?

ATL

Critical-thinking skills – Interpreting data

1 Study the graph showing the number of doctors per 1,000 people (Figure 1.4).
   - a Which countries had the highest number of doctors per 1,000 people in 2013?
   - b Which countries had the lowest number of doctors per 1,000 people in 2013?
   - c **Explain** the consequences for people of having i) a very low number of doctors per 1,000 people, and ii) a very high number of doctors per 1,000 people.

2 Study the political cartoon (Figure 1.5) 'The rich get richer and the poor get their byproducts'.
   - a **Describe** what is happening in the cartoon.
   - b **Explain** the message of the cartoon.
   - c Do you agree or disagree with the message? Why?

3 Study the table (Table 1.1) on endangered species.
   - a What do you understand by the term 'endangered'?
   - b **Explain** why certain species of animals are endangered.
   - c Choose one of the animals in the table to research in greater detail to find out more about the issue.

REFLECTION

In this section we have explored some examples of global issues. Write a reflection to **explain** what you understand about the issues facing the world and what you would like to find out more about.

Do some further research into one of the seven global issues presented on pages 6–7 to deepen your inquiry.

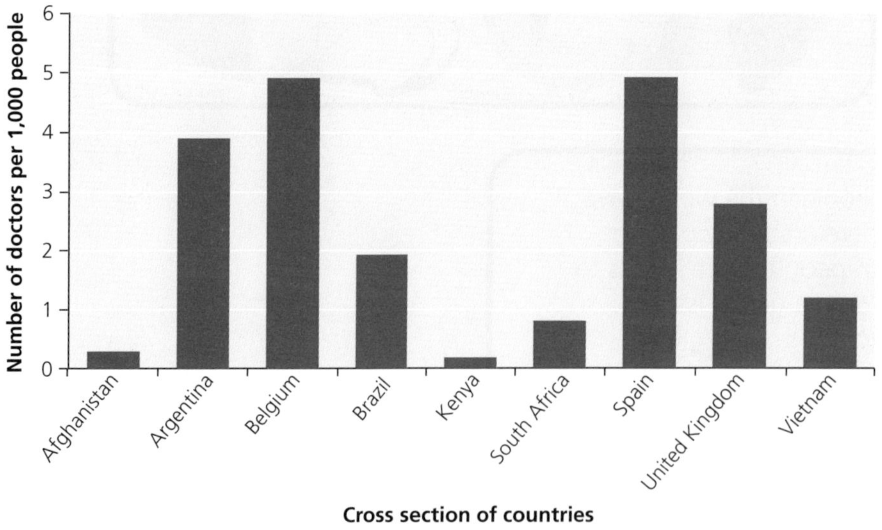

■ **Figure 1.4** Number of doctors per 1,000 people in 2013 (data from World Bank)

■ **Figure 1.5** A cartoon about the differences between the rich and the poor

■ **Table 1.1** Top ten endangered animals 2014 (data from World Wildlife Fund)

Species	Number left in the wild
Amur leopard	40
Javan rhinoceros	60
Panther	80
Red wolf	100
California condor	130
Sumatran rhinoceros	300
Cross River gorilla	300
Asiatic lion	350
Northern right whale	350
Indochinese tiger	500

How have different environments been damaged by human action?

■ **Figure 1.6** Plastic in the ocean

ENVIRONMENTAL CASE STUDY 1 – PLASTIC IN THE OCEANS

Plastic is a very useful product: it is cheap and easy to make and it lasts a long time. Plastic can be used to make a huge variety of products that have great benefit to people, including:

- bags
- chairs
- toys
- buttons
- water bottles
- shampoo bottles
- video game controllers
- light switches
- covering for wires
- keyboards.

■ **Figure 1.7** Worldwide, many billions of plastic water bottles are used every year

Despite these obvious uses, plastic is a problematic material for the environment. Much of the plastic waste in the world ends up in landfill sites or in the seas and oceans. As plastic takes a very long time to break down – and in many cases never completely degrades – this creates a major environmental issue. In recent years, environmentalists have been campaigning to raise more awareness of the consequences of the human use of plastic.

One of the places where you can often see the impact of the disposal of plastic is on the beaches. A huge variety of plastic can be found washed up on beaches across the world. For example, on a number of beaches in Hawaii, the plastic waste is so high that you actually need to dig into it to find decent amounts of sand. In addition, the vast majority of this plastic is not from Hawaii itself but has floated thousands of miles across the Pacific Ocean before reaching these beaches.

Environmentalists have found an area of the Pacific Ocean that they are calling the Great Pacific Garbage Patch. This is a vast area of the ocean, about the size of Texas, which is filled with plastic particles. It is found in an oceanic area called the doldrums, known for its calm winds, which in the past has trapped sailors for days when there has been no wind to power their boats.

▼ Links to: Sciences

The patterns of the tides in the seas and the oceans can create some interesting phenomena, which could be researched in your science classes. Explore the following terminology: doldrums, gyre, whirlpool. How can some of these tidal conditions help to explain the formation of the Great Pacific Garbage Patch?

SOURCE A

Account by Captain Charles Moore, discoverer of the Great Pacific Garbage Patch, in an article for Natural History *magazine in 2003*

'So on the way back to our home port in Long Beach, California, we decided to take a shortcut through the gyre, which few seafarers ever cross. Fishermen shun it because its waters lack the nutrients to support an abundant catch. Sailors dodge it because it lacks the wind to propel their sailboats.

'Yet as I gazed from the deck at the surface of what ought to have been a pristine ocean, I was confronted, as far as the eye could see, with the sight of plastic.

'It seemed unbelievable, but I never found a clear spot. In the week it took to cross the subtropical high, no matter what time of day I looked, plastic debris was floating everywhere: bottles, bottle caps, wrappers, fragments. Months later, after I discussed what I had seen with the oceanographer Curtis Ebbesmeyer, perhaps the world's leading expert on flotsam, he began referring to the area as the "eastern garbage patch".'

SOURCE C

Extract from the website of the National Resources Defense Council (NRDC), an environmental action group

'Plastic pollution affects every waterway, sea and ocean in the world. When we damage our water systems, we're putting our own well-being at risk. This pollution also has huge costs for taxpayers and local governments that must clean this trash off of beaches and streets to protect public health, prevent flooding from trash-blocked storm drains, and avoid lost tourism revenue from filthy beaches.'

SOURCE B

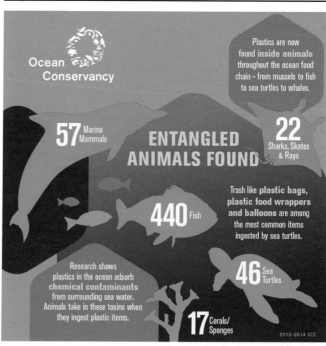

■ **Figure 1.8** The location of the Great Pacific Garbage Patch (convergence zone) and tidal currents

SOURCE D

■ **Figure 1.9** Top ten items found during the 2012 International Coastal Clean-up (data from Ocean Conservancy)

ACTIVITY: Plastic oceans

1 Why do you think plastic is such a widely used product?
2 According to the sources, why is plastic such a problem for the world's oceans and seas?
3 What is the Great Pacific Garbage Patch? Why does plastic get stuck there?
4 Why do you think Hawaii is particularly affected by these issues?
5 Copy and complete the following table.

Source	Origin	Purpose
A		
B		
C		
D		

6 **Circle of viewpoints** – in groups of six, take on one of the identities (see table).
   a In your groups, use the following scripts to **discuss** the plastic in the ocean issue using the different viewpoints.
     i I am thinking of the environmental impact of plastic from the point of view of …
     ii I think … (**Describe** the topic from your viewpoint. Be an actor – take on the character of your viewpoint.)
     iii A question I have from this viewpoint is … (**Ask** a question from this viewpoint.)

b After you have discussed the different viewpoints, choose three of the identities and write a paragraph for each to **explain** what you think their opinion would be about this global issue.

Environmental campaigner – You work for an environmental group that is committed to improving the environment. You regularly campaign about the state of the oceans and the seas.	**Chief Executive of a plastics company** – You run a major plastics manufacturing company that has been operating with high profits for many years. Many of your products end up in the seas and oceans.
Hotel owner at a beach resort – You are not usually too worried about environmental issues but you are concerned about how this issue might affect the beaches and water near the resort.	**Owner of a fishing boat** – You make a living through fishing. You have noticed that the amount of plastic debris in the ocean has increased over the years. You are unsure what to make of it.
Family living near the beach – You've lived by the coast for many years and enjoy going to the beach and swimming in the sea. You are seriously concerned about this issue.	**School student in a city** – You use a lot of plastic products in your daily life. You sometimes think about the environment but don't really think about the consequences of your actions.

◆ Assessment opportunities:

This activity can be assessed using Criterion D: Thinking critically (strands iii and iv).

Origin and purpose

What is meant by the origin and purpose of sources?

Within individuals and societies we often refer to different sources of information in terms of their **origin** and **purpose**. The origin of the source usually refers to where the information came from while the purpose considers the overall point of the information. The following questions can help you to understand what to write when asked about this:

Origin – What is the name of the source? Who made or wrote it? When was it made? Where was it created?

Purpose – Why was the source created? What is its intention? Who is it for?

For Criterion D: Thinking critically, one of the skills you need to develop is the clear identification of the origin and purpose of different sources.

WHAT ARE THE CONSEQUENCES OF PLASTIC IN THE OCEANS?

1 Harmful to wildlife

One of the most catastrophic consequences of plastic pollution is to wildlife. Marine animals can choke on pieces of plastic in the seas and oceans, often leading to death. Plastic can entangle animals causing them serious injury.

2 Environmental damage

A wide variety of environments can be affected by plastic pollution. As plastic does not break down easily it stays in the same place for a long time. The impact is evident on many beaches around the world, landfill sites and the collection of plastic in the oceans.

3 Plastic takes a long time to break down

The big problem of plastic pollution is getting it to break down. Plastic, unlike other materials, does not degrade fully. This means that if plastic is dropped as litter, it is likely to remain intact for a long time. Added to this problem is the throwaway culture in which plastic is often used. For instance, water bottles are often used only once and then thrown away, making these environmental issues more severe.

4 Health consequences for humans

Plastic can also be harmful to human health if it ends up in the food chain. Although research into the effects of plastic on human health is still in its early stages, there are concerns about how the scale of plastic in our natural environments will affect human health.

POLLUTION – As discussed in the case study, the disposal of plastic is a major pollutant affecting the seas and oceans, but there are many other materials deposited into waters causing other problems. As well as affecting marine life, pollution can also affect humans through consumption of fish. Particularly problematic pollutants include chemical fertilizers, sewage and oil.

What are some of the problems facing the seas and oceans?

OVER-FISHING – This is where an area of the ocean or sea is fished beyond its capability to recover the numbers of fish lost. This leads to major issues with the ecosystem.

GHOST FISHING – This is a problem caused by old fishing nets that are left in the seas after being discarded or lost by fishers. Different species of marine life get stuck in the nets, eventually leading to starvation or suffocation (see Figure 1.11).

SHARK FINNING – This issue affects sharks whose fins are sliced off to be used in shark fin soup. This practice has led to a number of species of shark becoming endangered; for instance, the hammerhead shark. The practice usually involves cutting the fins off the shark and then discarding the live shark back into the water, where it is unable to swim properly and at risk of suffocation.

■ **Figure 1.10** Some of the problems facing the seas and oceans

■ **Figure 1.11** Ghost fishing

WHAT ARE THE SOLUTIONS TO PLASTIC IN THE OCEANS?

1 Reduce

One of the easiest ways to improve the conditions of the environment due to plastic disposal is simply to use less plastic. Instead of purchasing single-use plastic water bottles, a reusable water bottle can significantly reduce wastage. By being more conscious of what we buy and how we dispose of it we can have positive effects on the environment.

2 Recycle

Plastic can be used more than once. Therefore, one way of reducing the impact of plastic use on the environment is through recycling. For instance, a plastic bag can be recycled and used numerous times for shopping. Plastic can be sorted for disposal and then recycled for different uses in local facilities.

3 Clean up

Another way to reduce the impact of plastic on the environment can be seen through efforts to actually clean it up. This can be done by individuals and local communities but also on national and global scales. Beach clean-ups are a good example of this in action.

4 Legal action

Governments hold huge power to help reduce the plastic problem. Laws can be passed which give people greater environmental responsibility. International organizations like the United Nations can also initiate more global responsibility towards the environment. Individuals can campaign to their local and national government representatives to take more action to improve environments.

5 Technology

New technologies could also be a solution by finding new products in the future or developing technology to clean up the seas and oceans. For information on some of these solutions visit this website: www.theoceancleanup.com

---

DISCUSS

'The oceans and seas are the shared responsibility of all countries.'

In groups, **discuss** this statement. Do you agree or disagree? What do you think are some of the major challenges with this concept? How do you think the issues affecting the ocean connect to the key concept of global interactions?

REFLECTION: Solutions

Copy and complete this table to reflect on possible solutions that could be carried out on a personal, local and global level.

Personal *What can I do as an individual to make a difference to this environmental issue?*	Local *What could my local community do to make a difference to this environmental issue?*	Global *What could national governments and global organizations do to make a difference to this environmental issue?*

ENVIRONMENTAL CASE STUDY 2 – DEFORESTATION

Deforestation refers to the loss of, and lack of replacement of, forests around the world. Trees can be replaced by replanting, but the speed of deforestation and the way the land is being used afterwards makes this a global issue. Deforestation occurs for a variety of reasons; often the land is cleared to make way for farms or the construction or extension of towns and cities. The trees themselves are valuable to many different industries where the wood can be used to make various products or for commercial purposes. Also, a lot of tree disposal is done through illegal logging, which is difficult to control.

SEE–THINK–WONDER

Look at Figure 1.13.

Why might the removal of trees create problems for the water cycle?

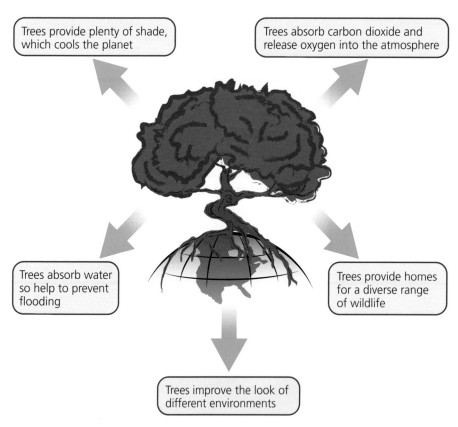

Trees provide plenty of shade, which cools the planet

Trees absorb carbon dioxide and release oxygen into the atmosphere

Trees absorb water so help to prevent flooding

Trees provide homes for a diverse range of wildlife

Trees improve the look of different environments

■ **Figure 1.12** The importance of trees

WHAT ARE THE CONSEQUENCES OF DEFORESTATION?

Disturbance to the water cycle

The **water cycle** refers to the movement of water on Earth. Trees play a crucial role in this cycle.

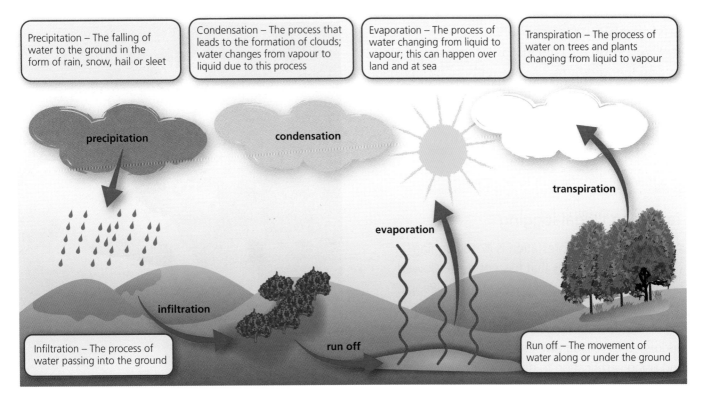

Precipitation – The falling of water to the ground in the form of rain, snow, hail or sleet

Condensation – The process that leads to the formation of clouds; water changes from vapour to liquid due to this process

Evaporation – The process of water changing from liquid to vapour; this can happen over land and at sea

Transpiration – The process of water on trees and plants changing from liquid to vapour

precipitation

condensation

transpiration

evaporation

infiltration

run off

Infiltration – The process of water passing into the ground

Run off – The movement of water along or under the ground

■ **Figure 1.13** The water cycle

Environmental consequences

Deforestation often takes place to make room for farming. A technique used to destroy large areas of forest is known as 'slash and burn'. This is a basic technique effectively burning away large areas of forest. The technique has been used throughout the history of farming but is widely criticized because of its negative effects on the environment. In 2013, there was a pollution crisis called the South East Asian Haze, which was thought to be caused by slash and burn techniques. Forested land was being targeted for burning in areas of Indonesia, which led to a haze that affected the air quality of numerous nearby countries.

Singapore reached its record level for air pollution during this time.

Trees also absorb carbon dioxide and give out oxygen. By reducing the number of trees in the world we are increasing the carbon dioxide level, thought to be a major cause of climate change.

Loss of homes

Trees are home to a huge variety of wildlife and there are also many human communities who live in forests and rely on them for their way of life. The destruction of rainforests has been seen to cause particularly acute issues for wildlife and tribal communities.

WHAT ARE SOME OF THE SOLUTIONS TO DEFORESTATION?

Sustainable practices

One solution to the issue of deforestation is the widespread use of more sustainable practices for cutting down the forests. Sustainability means having a balance within a system so it can last into the future. By replanting trees after others have been cut down and not clear-cutting huge areas, there is more chance of a manageable solution to this issue.

Targeting illegal logging

A key issue with deforestation is illegal logging. This is logging of trees that has not been allowed or sanctioned by a particular government. People do this to make quick profits without considering the environmental implications. This issue can be addressed by raising awareness of these practices and using certification to demonstrate that trees sold commercially have been cut down legally.

Reforestation

Another solution to deforestation is **reforestation**. That is, simply put, the replanting of trees on a large scale. This is designed to improve the atmosphere, to improve environments and to provide additional resources. It is also a technique to help to stop the spread of deserts. The Great Green Wall in the Sahara desert region of Africa, and the Green Wall of China are projects designed for this exact purpose. Some countries make reforestation a legal requirement to constantly improve the environment. There are also non-governmental organizations working at reforestation; one example of this is the Million Tree Project, which is part of the organization Roots and Shoots.

■ **Figure 1.14** Planting new trees on a large scale can help solve the problems caused by deforestation

Greening of urban areas

Many urban areas have parks within them, which make a big difference to the overall quality of the environment within the particular area. Governments can choose to plant more trees in urban areas to improve the environment. Innovative designs can be used to bring trees and greenery into unusual locations. For example, in New York City, the High Line Urban Park is a disused elevated railway line that has been converted into a green space. In Singapore, designers have pioneered vertical gardens, where greenery is grown up the side of buildings to improve the environment and bring about a range of benefits.

■ **Figure 1.15** The High Line Urban Park in New York City

ACTIVITY: Deforestation

■ ATL

Information literacy skills – Present information in a variety of formats and platforms

1 **Copy and complete the following table.**

List the reasons why deforestation is a global issue.	Explain the consequences of deforestation.	Reflect on the possible solutions to this issue.

The command terms for this task are highlighted below.

List – Give a sequence of brief answers with no explanation.

Explain – Give a detailed account including reasons or causes.

Reflect – Think about deeply; consider.

Definitions from IB MYP Individuals and societies guide, *2014*

2 **Design an infographic about deforestation. The infographic should use visuals to represent different facts about this global issue. The infographic could include the following:**
   ● **causes of deforestation**
   ● **consequences to the environment and people**
   ● **possible solutions.**

◆ Assessment opportunities:

In this activity you have practised skills that are assessed using Criterion A: Knowing and understanding and Criterion C: Communicating.

What are human rights?

Fundamental violations of human rights always leads to people feeling less and less human.

Aung San Suu Kyi

To deny people their human rights is to challenge their very humanity.

Nelson Mandela

The rights of every man are diminished when the rights of one man are threatened.

John F Kennedy

■ **Figure 1.16** What are human rights?

Freedom is a timeless value. The United Nations Charter calls for encouraging respect for fundamental freedoms. The Universal Declaration of Human Rights mentions freedom more than twenty times. All countries have committed to protecting individual freedoms on paper – but in practice, too many break their pledge.

Ban Ki-moon

THINK–PAIR–SHARE

What do you understand by the term 'human rights'?

Discuss the different messages of the quotations in Figure 1.16.

In the late 1940s, the world was still recovering from the extremities of the Second World War. The war had led to the death of many millions and had made the world more aware of the need for peace, cooperation and better rights and conditions for people. One of the organizations created as a result of the conflict was the United Nations (UN). The UN is an international organization committed to promoting peace, tolerance and cooperation among people across the world. One of the early developments of the UN was to publish a statement known as the Universal Declaration of Human Rights. This was presented in 1948 and is viewed by many as a foundation for how people should expect to be treated across the world. Subsequently, it is often referred to when considering the topic of human rights.

UNIVERSAL DECLARATION OF HUMAN RIGHTS

SIMPLIFIED VERSION

This simplified version of the 30 Articles of the Universal Declaration of Human Rights has been created especially for young people.

1 We are all born free and equal.	We are all born free. We all have our own thoughts and ideas. We should all be treated in the same way.
2 Don't discriminate.	These rights belong to everybody, whatever our differences.
3 The right to life.	We all have the right to life, and to live in freedom and safety.
4 No slavery.	Nobody has any right to make us a slave. We cannot make anyone our slave.
5 No torture.	Nobody has any right to hurt us or to torture us.
6 You have rights no matter where you go.	I am a person just like you!
7 We are all equal before the law.	The law is the same for everyone. It must treat us all fairly.
8 Your human rights are protected by law.	We can all ask for the law to help us when we are not treated fairly.
9 No unfair detainment.	Nobody has the right to put us in prison without good reason and keep us there, or to send us away from our country.
10 The right to trial.	If we are put on trial this should be in public. The people who try us should not let anyone tell them what to do.
11 We are always innocent till proven guilty.	Nobody should be blamed for doing something until it is proven. When people say we did a bad thing we have the right to show it is not true.
12 The right to privacy.	Nobody should try to harm our good name. Nobody has the right to come into our home, open our letters, or bother us or our family without a good reason.
13 Freedom to move.	We all have the right to go where we want in our own country and to travel as we wish.
14 The right to seek a safe place to live.	If we are frightened of being badly treated in our own country, we all have the right to run away to another country to be safe.
15 Right to a nationality.	We all have the right to belong to a country.

■ **Figure 1.17** Simplified version of the Universal Declaration of Human Rights

ACTIVITY: Human rights cartoon strip

■ ATL

Creative-thinking skills – Create original works and ideas; use existing works and ideas in new ways

Create a cartoon strip based on one of the rights from the list (Figure 1.17). The cartoon strip should **summarize**, through a story with characters, an example of one of the rights being broken and should **explain** the features of the particular right.

What are some of the human rights issues facing children?

Unfortunately, there are still a range of human rights issues across the world that affect people in different ways. One group that is particularly at threat is children. Children can often be seen to be more at risk from human rights abuses as they are more vulnerable members of society. In many parts of the world, children are employed to work in factories or on farms, often having to work for hours on end without free time to play with friends or rest. Issues with child labour tend to be worse in poorer countries where children are often relied on to bring income into a household. They may be helping their parents by working on farms, or collecting food and water from different areas.

Some children are even recruited to work as soldiers and face very difficult conditions. Despite international efforts to reduce this practice, there are still children working as soldiers. Often they are trained to kill and may experience violence towards themselves including torture and sexual abuse.

There are multiple organizations working to raise awareness of the conditions facing children around the world. The United Nations International Children's Emergency Fund (UNICEF), for instance, is committed to working to improve human rights and conditions for children globally. Conditions for children can suddenly worsen if a war or natural disaster strikes. Children can often be left displaced, without a home or sometimes without parents. This puts them at high risk in particular societies.

SOURCE A

Myint Khine, aged 17, speaking about his experiences as a child soldier in Myanmar

'"They put me in a pitch black cell, scraped my shins and electrocuted me... they tied me up and electrocuted my legs and if that did not work, they would scrape my legs again.

"They would then force me to kneel on broken glass with my arms in an airplane position. The worst thing is that they would beat me with a stick after this... until I fell unconscious.

"They would shove a huge piece of fish and chili paste in my mouth and I had to hold it... I wanted to commit suicide. I just wanted to die."

'Myint Khine claims he was forced to serve in the state armed forces by recruitment officials, who used his father's politically active background as a threat against him and his family. He said that prior to being conscripted he was detained and severely tortured for six months because of his family background. He was made to serve in the army despite his poor eyesight and chronic health problems.'

EXTENSION

Do some research into the work of UNICEF and **explore** the different issues that it is campaigning for. **Investigate** the ways in which you can make a difference.

SOURCE B

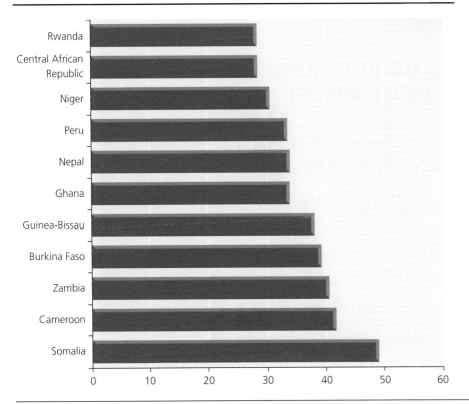

ACTIVITY: Source investigation

■ ATL

Information literacy skills – Access information to be informed and inform others

1   According to Source A and Source C, what are some of the difficulties experienced by Myint and Alejandra?
2   Look at the graph in Figure 1.18. What information does the graph give us? Why may poorer (or developing) countries be more likely to have higher levels of child labour?

■ **Figure 1.18** Percentage of children between the ages of 5 and 14 employed in child labour; 10 highest countries (data from UNICEF 2014)

SOURCE C

Description of a child worker's typical day collecting molluscs from a swamp in El Salvador

'Twelve-year-old Alejandra is woken up at four in the morning by her father, Don José. She does not go to school, but goes to collect curiles, small molluscs in the mangrove swamps on the island of Espiritu Santo in Usulutan, El Salvador.

'In the rush to get to work, Alejandra does not take time to eat breakfast. It is more important to make sure she has the things she needs to make it through a workday that can mean spending up to 14 hours in the mud. These items include about a dozen cigars and at least four pills to keep her from falling asleep. A good part of the money that she earns goes to buy these things.

'In the mangrove swamp without shoes, Alejandra has to face bad weather, mosquito bites and cuts and scrapes from having to pull the curiles out from deep in the mud. The cigars help to repel the mosquitoes, but when she runs out of cigars Alejandra has to put up with the insects as she moves from branch to branch and from one area to another in search of shells. When she returns from work, her body is nearly always covered with bites.

'She earns very little. If she is lucky in one day Alejandra manages to collect two baskets of curiles (150 shells), worth little more than 12 colones, or $1.40. Alejandra, who has seven younger brothers and sisters, has no time to go to school or play with other children. Anyway, she prefers not to play with other children because they say she smells bad and exclude her from their games for being a curiles worker. Little by little Alejandra has lost her self-esteem. Like the other children who work collecting curiles, she feels separate from the rest of society. For Alejandra, life seems like a tunnel with no exit.'

CASE STUDY – THE UNITED NATIONS GLOBAL GOALS FOR SUSTAINABLE DEVELOPMENT

In September 2015, the UN launched the Global Goals, a set of targets for the world over the next 15 years (Figure 1.19). The aims of these goals include ending extreme poverty, tackling climate change and getting rid of inequality.

Although launched by an international organization, the only way that these goals can be successful is if there is action by individuals, organizations and governments around the world to commit to these practices.

■ **Figure 1.19** Global Goals for Sustainable Development from the UN

SUMMATIVE ASSESSMENT TASK: Presentation on an issue facing your local community

■ **ATL**

- Communication skills – Use a variety of
  speaking techniques to communicate with a
  variety of audiences
- Critical-thinking skills – Gather and organize
  relevant information to formulate an
  argument

Create a presentation on an issue in your local
community. Think about some of the issues
facing your local area; it could be environmental
or it could be to do with people. Within your
presentation, clearly **identify** what the issue is.

Steps for completing the task:

1 **Identify** the issue (think about your local area,
   talk to your family and friends to **identify** an
   issue that you think needs attention).
2 **Research** the issue (start to take notes on
   why you think it is an issue, think about the
   causes and consequences).
3 **Collect evidence (this could be photographs,
   interviews with members of your community,
   secondary research through online sources
   or books).**

4 **Create** your presentation (remember to
   include evidence to support your points. Keep
   it visual to engage your audience).
5 **Present your work to your teacher and peers.**

Examples of issues in a local community that you
could you focus on:
- **litter problem and recycling schemes**
- **beach clean-ups**
- **school environments**
- **healthy eating**
- **facilities for disabled people**
- **conditions for the elderly**
- **prejudice and/or discrimination in your
  community**
- **pollution problems, traffic.**

◆ Assessment opportunities:

This activity can be assessed using Criterion B:
Investigating (strands iii and iv) and Criterion C:
Communicating (strands i and ii).

Creating a questionnaire

Questionnaires are extremely useful for gathering evidence that you can use in different assignments. Creating a questionnaire usually involves writing up a list of questions that are answered by a cross section of people. This task is a good opportunity to practise creating questionnaires to find out about conditions in your local community.

Hints for creating questionnaires

- Try to include different types of questions.
- Try to sample a relatively large number of people.
- Try to sample people of different ages.
- Think about the quality of your questions.

Different types of questions – qualitative and quantitative

Qualitative questions are open-ended questions where the person answering can say what they think in answer to the question. For instance:

What do you think are the issues facing our local community?

or

Write down five words to describe your personality.

They are not looking for a fixed response.

Quantitative questions, on the other hand, are questions that ask for a specific response that can be measured and subsequently turned into a graph. For instance:

Please rate our local community's recycling schemes from 1 to 5.

1 Excellent   2 Good   3 Satisfactory   4 Poor   5 Very poor

or

How often do you recycle your household waste? Circle the response that best fits.

Always   Often   Sometimes   Rarely

By thinking about the quality and type of the questions that are written, questionnaires can be a great way of collecting evidence in Individuals and Societies.

REFLECTION: How can individuals make a difference to others?

Create a mind map to answer the question 'How can individuals make a difference to others?' Think about a range of different ways that individuals can take action. Once you have completed your mind map, share your ideas with others in your class.

! Take action

Create a simulation role play based on a human rights issue. Put this together as a drama production to show to your school community to raise awareness of the human rights issue.

Reflection

As we have seen, there are many issues affecting people and the planet that we live on. There are solutions to promote positive change, but for this to happen individuals are required to take action and to view themselves as global citizens.

Use this table to reflect on your own learning in this chapter		
Questions we asked	Answers we found	Any further questions now?
Factual What are some of the issues facing the world today? How have different environments been damaged by human action? What are some of the human rights issues facing children? What is the role of international organizations in tackling global issues?		
Conceptual What is meant by the term 'human rights'?		
Debatable Can individuals change the world?		

Approaches to learning you used in this chapter	Description – what new skills did you learn?	How well did you master the skills?			
		Novice	Learner	Practitioner	Expert
Communication skills					
Creative-thinking skills					
Critical-thinking skills					
Information literacy skills					

Learner profile attribute(s)	Reflect on the importance of caring for your learning in this chapter.
Caring	

2 How can maps provide us with a sense of time, place and space?

○ Maps provide insights into **time, place and space and show how the world has changed over time,** but they can be affected by different **perspectives.**

■ **Figure 2.1** Maps are ofter used to help us find our way. What else could a map be used for?

CONSIDER THESE QUESTIONS:

Factual: What are maps? What are the different types of maps? What are the different features of maps and how can we use them? How is height represented on a map?

Conceptual: How do maps help us to understand time, place and space?

Debatable: Can we always trust maps?

Now **share and compare** your thoughts and ideas with your partner, or with the whole class.

○ IN THIS CHAPTER, WE WILL ...

■ **Find out** about the different uses of maps, as well as how they can be affected by a specific perspective.

■ **Explore** different examples of maps and how to use them.

■ **Take action** by considering the ways that maps can communicate important information.

These Approaches to Learning (ATL) skills will be useful …

■ These Approaches to Learning (ATL) skills will be useful …

- Communication skills
- Creative-thinking skills
- Critical-thinking skills
- Information literacy skills
- Reflection skills

● We will reflect on this learner profile attribute …

Knowledgeable – developing understanding of mapping by exploring different types of maps and how to use them.

◆ Assessment opportunities in this chapter:

- **Criterion A:** Knowing and understanding
- **Criterion B:** Investigating
- **Criterion C:** Communicating
- **Criterion D:** Thinking critically

KEY WORDS

cartography	scale
contour lines	topographic
grid references	

THINK–PAIR–SHARE

In pairs, write down your own definition of a map, and then try to think of as many different uses of maps as you can. Share your ideas. When was the last time you used a map?

What are maps?

Maps are visual representations of specific areas; they come in many different forms, shapes and sizes. They are used to communicate information about the location and look of the different things within that specific area. Maps can be very useful to help to gain a sense of direction and size and to understand the different features that might be in that particular area. They can also be used to communicate a specific feature of a location such as population size or the amount of natural resources available.

The study of maps and the work involved in creating them is known as **cartography**, and people who make maps are called cartographers. In this chapter we will explore examples of different maps and how to use them as well as how maps can be affected by specific perspectives.

■ **Figure 2.2** Some examples of different types of maps: (a) a map of the Shire from Lord of the Rings, (b) a mobile travel map, (c) Charles Booth's Poverty Map, (d) Stephen Walter's London Etching

WHAT ARE THE DIFFERENT TYPES OF MAPS?

As mentioned above, there are many different types of maps. Figure 2.3 shows a selection of different types of maps that you might come across in daily life (see pages 32–33).

ACTIVITY: Different types of maps

■ ATL

Critical-thinking skills – Revise understanding based on new information and evidence

1 Use the information in Figure 2.3 to work out which type of map you would need to find out the information in the following scenarios:
   a The route for a motorist to drive from Rome to Florence in Italy.
   b The capital cities of Europe.
   c Aerial footage of the shape and size of Africa.
   d The different features of the outback in Australia.
   e The comparative population sizes of countries in South East Asia.
   f The height of the Rocky Mountains in the USA.
2 Look at the map in Figure 2.4. Answer these questions:
   a What information does this map give us?
   b Who would find this map useful and why?
   c Does this map have any limitations?

DISCUSS

When was the last time you used a map?

EXTENSION

Explore these interactive and digital maps:

http://lotrproject.com/map/#zoom=3&lat=-1334&lon=1500&layers=BTTTTT

www.bl.uk/magnificentmaps/map4.html

POLITICAL

These maps show features that have been created by governments. For example, a political map may show official national boundaries, capital cities and towns.

TOPOGRAPHIC

These maps are very detailed and show both physical and political features. They are noted for the use of **contour lines** that provide information about the height of the ground above sea level.

DATA AND RESOURCE

These maps provide information on a specific resource and/or statistical information. For example, the map could show climate, population size, or the availability of natural resources.

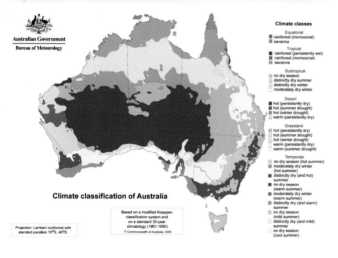

PHYSICAL

These maps show the physical characteristics of the land and water in a particular area. For instance, physical maps can show details about mountains, rivers and desert areas.

■ **Figure 2.3** Types of maps

ROAD

Road maps are more localized maps that show detailed transport routes. They are typically used for navigation purposes by motorists.

SATELLITE

These show images of different areas taken from a satellite. They tend to be very accurate and detailed.

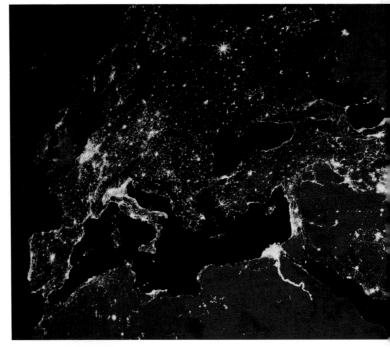

■ **Figure 2.4** A satellite map of Europe and Africa

EXTENSION

Research other types of maps not mentioned in the chapter; for example, geological, historical and weather maps.

How do we use maps?

Maps have a range of features that help us to understand how they work and how to use them. The following features are common to most maps.

DIRECTION

Direction or orientation is usually represented on a map by the use of a compass rose. This shows the directions in real life on the map. The directional points on a compass rose are called **cardinal points** and are north, south, east and west, represented as N, S, E, W.

ACTIVITY: Direction

■ ATL

Communication skills – Use and interpret a range of discipline-specific terms and symbols

Using the compass rose and Figure 2.5, answer the following questions.

1 If Poppy travels to Fraser's house, in what direction does she travel?
2 If Sebastian travels to Poppy's house, in what direction does he travel?
3 If Fraser travels to Sebastian's house, in what direction does he travel?
4 If Wendy travels first to Sebastian's house and then travels to Fraser's house, in which two directions will she have travelled?

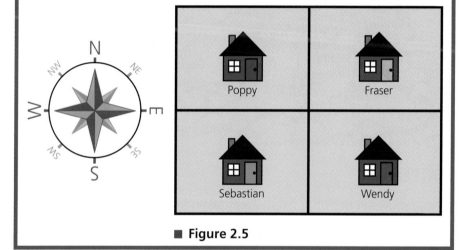

■ **Figure 2.5**

ⓘ Using a compass

When reading a map, a physical compass can be used to correlate the direction in the map to real life. Compasses, as well as being equipped with cardinal points, are also numbered from 0 to 360 degrees.

■ **Figure 2.6** Using a compass

North = 0 degrees   South = 180 degrees

East = 90 degrees   West = 270 degrees

Some compasses show eight points including north-east (NE), south-east (SE), south-west (SW) and north-west (NW). This allows you to be more accurate when describing direction.

Compasses that are used with maps have a magnetic needle that points to magnetic north. This means that when out hiking or orienteering in the countryside, you can use a map and a compass to find the direction in which you need to travel.

Search **How to use a baseplate compass** for more information on using a compass.

SCALE

Scale is very important when reading a map; it allows you to understand the size of a particular area in real life. The scale tells you the level of reduction that the map shows in comparison to real life. Scale is often represented in linear form. This type of scale depicts the real-world distance along a line.

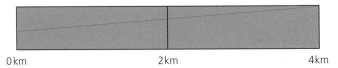

0 km   2 km   4 km

■ **Figure 2.7** Scale bar

Scale can also be represented as a written sentence or a ratio. For instance:

     1 cm represents 2 km (1:200 000)

or

     1 cm represents 500 m (1:50 000)

When working out the actual distance from a map you need to use a ruler to measure the distance between places on the map and then use the scale to calculate the actual distance on the ground.

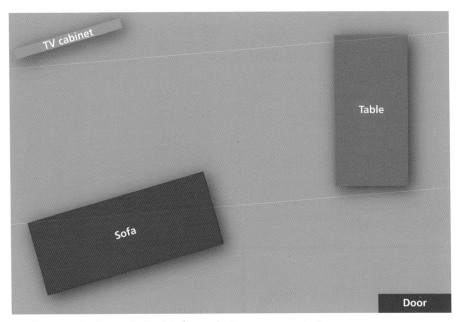

■ **Figure 2.8** The scale in this figure is 2 cm represents 1 m

---

2   How can maps provide us with a sense of time, place and space?   35

ACTIVITY: Getting to know scale

■ ATL

Communication skills – Understand and use mathematical notation

Using Figure 2.8, answer the following questions.

1 **What is the actual distance between the TV and the sofa?**
2 **What is the actual distance between the door and the table?**
3 **What is the surface area of the table?**
4 **Write out the scale of this diagram in a) linear form and b) ratio form.**
5 **Create your own scale drawing of a room in your home or your classroom. Make sure you include an appropriate scale.**

▼ Links to: Maths and design

As well as being extremely useful for creating maps, scale is also used in modelling and architecture. Scaled-down models allow designers to test out different versions of their products to see if they will work in reality. Think about a practical scale you would need to use in order to create scaled-down models of the following: an airplane, a skyscraper and a boat.

ACTIVITY: Symbols on a map

1 **Look at the symbols in Figure 2.9. What do you think they would represent on a map?**

■ **Figure 2.9** Typical examples of symbols on a map

2 **Imagine you are creating a map of your school. Think of five things that would need to be represented as a symbol on the map. Draw the symbols and write what they represent.**

SYMBOLS

Maps contain symbols to represent different things. The symbols are placed together in a **key** to show their different meanings. A wide variety of things are represented in this way.

GRID REFERENCES

Grid references refer to a specific position on a map. They can be usually written as either a **four-figure grid reference** or a **six-figure grid reference**.

Four-figure grid references are worked out by first locating the object along the horizontal axis, and second along the vertical axis. Consequently, in Figure 2.10, the four-figure grid reference for the letter P would be **1202**. The 12 is from the horizontal axis and the 02 is from the vertical axis. One way to remember how to work out four-figure grid references is the analogy of first going into the house and then up the stairs: walk along the horizontal axis first and then up the vertical axis.

Six-figure grid references are a little bit more complicated. To do this, we need to imagine that each box is divided into ten parts. Once again, we go along the horizontal axis first and then up the vertical axis. In Figure 2.11, therefore, S would have a six-figure grid reference of **124007**.

DISCUSS

What are the four-figure and six-figure grid references for Q and R in Figure 2.10?

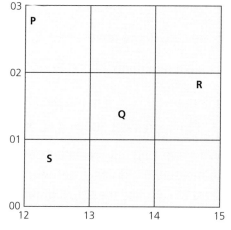

■ **Figure 2.10** Using four-figure grid references

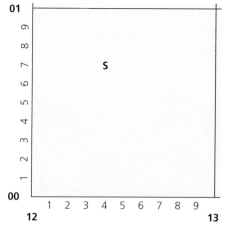

■ **Figure 2.11** Using six-figure grid references

ACTIVITY: Island getaway

Information literacy skills – Make connections between various sources of information

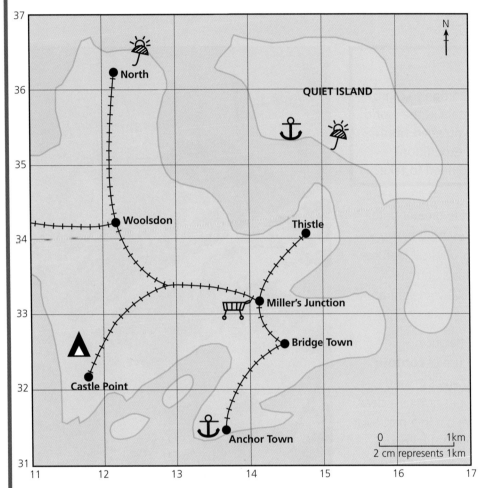

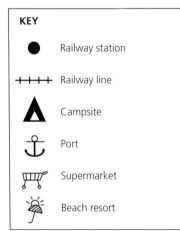

KEY

● Railway station

+|+|+ Railway line

▲ Campsite

⚓ Port

🛒 Supermarket

Beach resort

■ **Figure 2.12**

Look at the map (Figure 2.12) and answer the following questions.

1 In what direction would you be travelling if you travelled from Anchor Town to Bridge Town?
2 What is the four-figure grid reference of the beach resort near North Point?
3 What is the four-figure grid reference of the port on Quiet Island?
4 If you travelled by train from North Point to Miller's Junction, in which two directions would you be travelling?

5 What is the six-figure grid reference of **a)** the campsite by Castle Point; **b)** the port at Anchor Town; **c)** the supermarket at Miller's Junction; **d)** Thistle Head railway station?
6 What is the actual (shortest) distance between the port at Anchor Town and the port on Quiet Island?
7 By rail, how far would you travel if you took the most direct route between Woolsdon and Bridge Town?
8 Write out the scale for this map as a ratio.

How is height represented on a map?

Physical and topographic maps provide greater detail on the actual shape of the land represented by showing information about different physical features in a landscape such as rivers, mountains and the coastline. The maps also show the relative height above sea level of features.

One of the most common ways that height is represented on a map is through the use of **contour lines**. These lines are used to indicate areas of land that have the same height. Contour lines give us a clear indication of how steep or how flat land is in a particular area; this variation in the height of the land is known as **relief**. For instance, areas on a map with numerous contour lines close together are a clear indication of steep slopes, whereas an area of a map with relatively few contour lines is likely to be more flat. The distance between the contour lines is called the **contour interval** and this will be the same for the whole map.

As well as elevation, contour lines can be used to measure depth, and they can be used on oceanic maps, which chart the depths of the seabed.

■ **Figure 2.13** Mount Everest

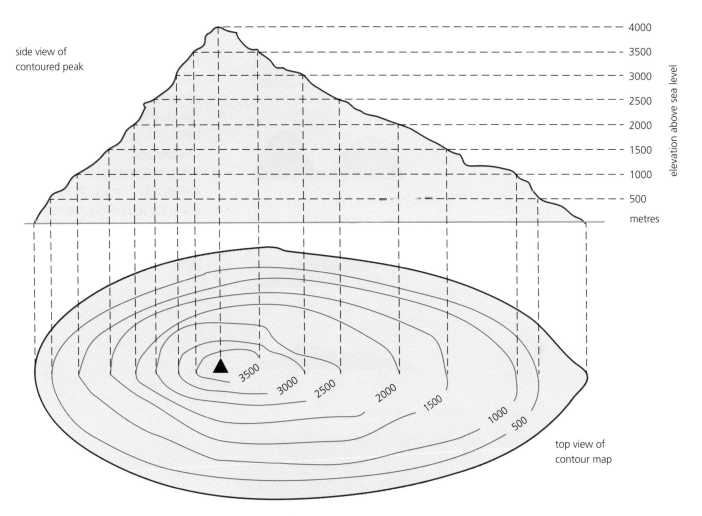

side view of
contoured peak

elevation above sea level

4000
3500
3000
2500
2000
1500
1000
500
metres

3500
3000
2500
2000
1500
1000
500

top view of
contour map

■ **Figure 2.14** How a peak or mountain would look on a contour map

THINK–PAIR–SHARE

Why might some people want to create maps to
show the depths of the seas and oceans?

2   How can maps provide us with a sense of time, place and space?

39

ACTIVITY: How is height represented on a map?

■ ATL

Communication skills – Use and interpret a range of discipline-specific terms and symbols

1

2

3

4

a

b

c

d

■ **Figure 2.15** Matching contour maps to cross sections

Study the photograph (Figure 2.16a) and the map (Figure 2.16b) and then answer the following questions.

1 **Match up the cross sections to the contour maps in Figure 2.15.**
2 **Using the details on the photograph, pinpoint on the map where you would be standing if you took this photograph.**
3 **Using the map, plan a hike from Wilkinsyke Farm to Honnister Crag. Describe the route and terrain you are likely to come across as you complete the hike.**

■ **Figure 2.16a** View of Buttermere from Fleetwith Pike in the Lake District, UK

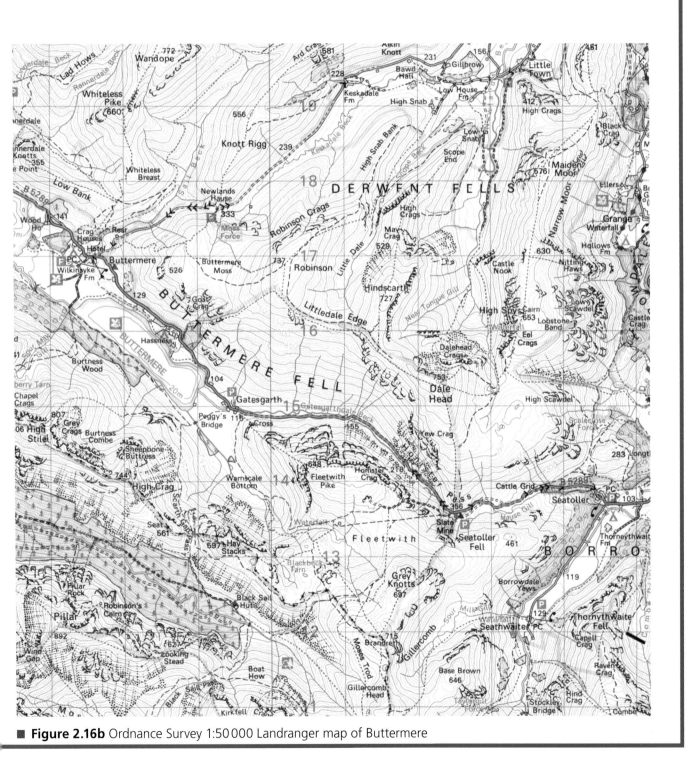

■ **Figure 2.16b** Ordnance Survey 1:50 000 Landranger map of Buttermere

How can maps help us to understand time, place and space?

Maps provide a range of insights into different locations and they can deepen our understanding of time, place and space.

TIME

- Historic maps can help us to see what locations would have looked like at different times in the past. For instance, a map of London in the 1920s would look significantly different from a contemporary map.
- Maps can also be created of future planned developments; for example, a map of a new city. Therefore, maps can also help us to visualize something before it exists.

PLACE

- Maps give a detailed understanding of place by showing the different features of the location.
- These features can include the land use, buildings and natural features.
- The use of a key on a map provides a range of details about the place that can be quickly understood; for instance, the number of restaurants in a town.

SPACE

- Maps also provide an insight into space through the use of scale, direction and elevation.
- Scale allows the reader of the map to be able to interpret the map to understand the actual distance on the ground.
- Direction allows the reader of the map to understand the orientation of certain features in a location or in which direction to travel to get from one place to another.
- The elevation provides an insight into the land height as well as other physical features such as the height above sea level, or the amount of flat land.

ACTIVITY: Hypothetical maps

■ ATL

Critical-thinking skills – Draw reasonable conclusions and generalizations

1 Consider the following hypothetical maps. For each map write down what it could tell us about time, place and space.
   a A political map of Qing Dynasty China in the nineteenth century.
   b An architect's designs and map of a new suburb planned to be built on the outskirts of Cape Town in South Africa.
   c A detailed physical and topographic map of Yellowstone National Park in the USA.
2 How do you think the following people would use maps as part of their work: a) a geologist; b) a historian; c) a taxi driver; d) a government official; e) a police officer?

Bias

Bias is a term used to describe information that seems to take a particular side or viewpoint. For instance, a newspaper may be biased towards a particular political viewpoint and always portray issues through that opinion.

Maps are less likely to have bias but may be affected by a variety of factors during their creation; for example, the information available; the purpose of the map; any political considerations. Maps sometimes have to show disputed borders between nations; this is often a problem for cartographers. However, it is important to remember that biased sources of information are still very useful and they can provide an important insight into a particular viewpoint.

Can we always trust maps?

Despite their varied uses in everyday life, maps can be affected by a range of perspectives. This means at times we need to consider their representation carefully.

An example of this can be found in the debate between the Mercator and Gall-Peters world maps. Both versions are of the world stretched out in a two-dimensional (2D) format. Given the fact that the Earth is a sphere (3D) not 2D, it means that there are some inevitable inaccuracies. The Mercator, the more widely used approach, dates back to the work of the Flemish cartographer Geradus Mercator in the late sixteenth century. He sought to map the world, especially with the intention of helping people to navigate the seas for exploration and trade.

The Gall-Peters projection is attributed to both the early work of James Gall in the mid-nineteenth century and Arno Peters in the late 1960s. This map projection offered a version of the world where the actual sizes of places in the world are directly proportional to their sizes on the map. This made it more convincing to some people given the inaccuracies of the Mercator projection, such as the distorted size of the polar regions.

The Mercator versus Gall-Peters debate raises an important point about how maps can present a particular perspective or world view. Maps can also be affected by political issues or disputes; for example, disputed borders between two or more countries. Disputes of this nature make it difficult to construct accurate political maps as the borders can change over time. Maps can also be created to suit a nation's interests so may be less accurate in terms of the information that is presented.

■ **Figure 2.17** Mercator projection

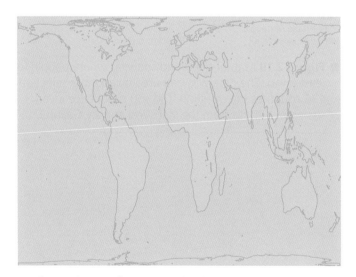

■ **Figure 2.18** Gall-Peters projection

DISCUSS

Look at the two maps (Figures 2.17 and 2.18). In pairs, **list** of the some of the similarities and differences between the two maps. **Discuss** the advantages and disadvantages of each projection.

SOURCE A

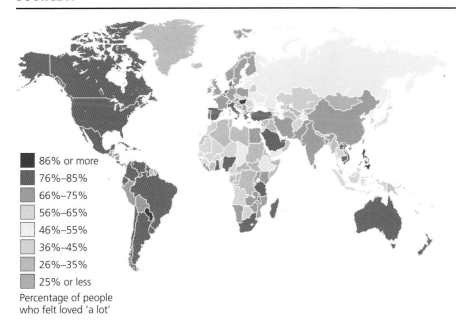

86% or more
76%–85%
66%–75%
56%–65%
46%–55%
36%–45%
26%–35%
25% or less

Percentage of people
who felt loved 'a lot'

■ **Figure 2.19** Map of the world showing where people feel the most and least loved. The data was gathered by asking a selection of people in 136 countries the question 'Did you experience love for a lot of the day yesterday?' (Data from the statistical agency Gallup.)

SOURCE B

Extract about borders from National Geographic *magazine*

'A border is a real or artificial line that separates geographic areas. Borders are political boundaries. They separate countries, states, provinces, counties, cities, and towns. A border outlines the area that a particular governing body controls. The government of a region can only create and enforce laws within its borders.

'Borders change over time. Sometimes the people in one region take over another area through violence. Other times, land is traded or sold peacefully. Many times, land is parceled out after a war through international agreements.

'Sometimes, borders fall along natural boundaries like rivers or mountain ranges. For example, the boundary between France and Spain follows the crest of the Pyrenees mountains. For part of its length, the boundary between the United States and Mexico follows a river called the Rio Grande. The borders of four countries divide Africa's Lake Chad: Niger, Chad, Cameroon, and Nigeria.'

SOURCE C

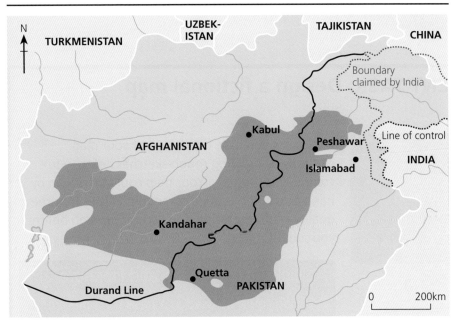

■ **Figure 2.20** Map showing the Durand Line border between Afghanistan and Pakistan, a border that was established between Britain and Afghanistan during the late nineteenth century, when the Indian subcontinent (including Pakistan) was part of the British Empire. When Pakistan became an independent state in 1947 it questioned the legitimacy of the border. Afghanistan and Pakistan have disputed the border frequently since then.

ACTIVITY: Can we always trust maps?

■ **ATL**

Critical-thinking skills – Draw reasonable conclusions and generalizations

1 Study Source A carefully. What does the map tell us? Why might this information be useful to people? Can you think of any limitations of this map?

2 According to Source B, what are some of the reasons why borders change over time? What issues might this bring about when using or making maps?

3 What does Source C suggest about the ways that maps can be used to explore historical time periods and events?

4 Using the sources and your own knowledge, write a detailed response to the following question: '**Can we always trust maps?**'

◆ Assessment opportunities:

This activity can be assessed using Criterion D: Thinking critically (strands i and ii).

SUMMATIVE ASSESSMENT TASK: Design a fictional map and written reflection

PART ONE

For this assessment task you will need to **demonstrate** your understanding of mapping by creating your own fictional map. You can be creative with the design of your map but you need to use a range of conventions within your map to **demonstrate** your understanding.

Your map needs to include the following features:
- a title
- a scale
- direction
- a key for the symbols on the map
- grid references
- physical features (eg rivers, mountains).

Spend some time researching examples of fictional maps in works of literature (for example, the *Lord of the Rings* books) to give you an idea of how you can use your imagination to create a really interesting map.

Make sure you plan the design of your map carefully by drawing rough sketches before you complete it properly. Your map could be drawn by hand or created using a computer. Ensure that the quality of presentation and accuracy is high before you submit it.

▼ Links to: Language and literature

The map could be used as a basis for a piece of creative writing where the places constructed in the map are brought to life in a story.

PART TWO

Produce a written reflection of the process of designing and creating the map. Think about the following questions:
- **What ideas did you have and why did you decide on this design?**
- **What went well?**
- **What didn't go as planned?**
- **What would you do differently next time?**

◆ Assessment opportunities:

This activity can be assessed using Criterion A: Knowing and understanding (strands i and ii), Criterion B: Investigating (strand iv) and Criterion C: Communicating (strands i and ii).

Reflection

In this chapter, we have explored a range of different types of maps as well as the different ways in which they can be used. These skills help us to recognize the importance of maps and how they can provide an insight into time, place and space. It is important to remember that maps may be affected by a particular perspective, but that does not necessarily affect their value as a source of information.

Use this table to reflect on your own learning in this chapter		
Questions we asked	Answers we found	Any further questions now?
Factual What are maps? What are the different types of maps? What are the different features of maps and how can we use them? How is height represented on a map?		
Conceptual How do maps help us to understand time, place and space?		
Debatable Can we always trust maps?		

Approaches to learning you used in this chapter	Description – what new skills did you learn?	How well did you master the skills?			
		Novice	Learner	Practitioner	Expert
Communication skills					
Creative-thinking skills					
Critical-thinking skills					
Information literacy skills					
Reflection skills					
Learner profile attribute(s)	Reflect on the importance of being knowledgeable for your learning in this chapter.				
Knowledgeable					

3 What can we learn from different civilizations?

○ Civilizations have developed at different **times and locations** bringing about **change** and **innovation** that often influence **how we view them today**.

CONSIDER THESE QUESTIONS:

Factual: What were the achievements of the Sumerian and Egyptian civilizations? What were the major contributions of the Greek civilization? How did the Roman civilization change over time? What has been the legacy of the Roman civilization? What were the features of the Maya and Inca civilizations?

Conceptual: How can we find out about the past? What is a civilization? What factors led to the emergence and achievements of different civilizations?

Debatable: Is it possible to ever know the past?

Now **share and compare** your thoughts and ideas with your partner, or with the whole class.

■ **Figure 3.1** Temple of Jaguar, Tikal, Guatemala

○ IN THIS CHAPTER, WE WILL ...

- **Find out** about different civilizations that emerged at different times in history.
- **Explore** the factors that led to the development and innovations of different civilizations.
- **Take action** by finding out ways that historical sites and artefacts can be protected for the future.

ACTIVITY: Historical treasures

ACTIVITY: Historical treasures

■ ATL

Creative-thinking skills – Use brainstorming and visual diagrams to generate new ideas and inquiries

In pairs, look through the following list of famous historical sites in the world:
- **Pyramids at Giza, Egypt**
- **Machu Picchu, Peru**
- **Great Wall of China**
- **Coliseum, Italy**
- **Petra, Jordan**
- **Angkor Wat, Cambodia**
- **Stonehenge, UK**
- **Parthenon, Greece**
- **Taj Mahal, India**
- **Tikal, Guatemala**

Discuss the following questions: How many have you heard of? Why do you think they are famous? What do they suggest about different societies in the past? Why could it be useful to learn about past societies and civilizations?

■ These Approaches to Learning (ATL) skills will be useful …

- Communication skills
- Creative-thinking skills
- Critical-thinking skills
- Information literacy skills
- Reflection skills

● We will reflect on this learner profile attribute …

Inquirer – inquiring into examples of different historic civilizations and developing our own ideas and understanding about their significance.

◆ Assessment opportunities in this chapter:

- **Criterion A:** Knowledge and understanding
- **Criterion C:** Communicating
- **Criterion D:** Thinking critically

KEY WORDS

civilization	philosophy
governance	public health
hieroglyphics	democracy

The achievements of past civilizations can be seen in the various artefacts and historical sites left in the world today that provide a window into their world. From the pyramids of Ancient Egypt through to the network of roads built by the Roman Empire, these remains help us to understand what life would have been like in different societies many years ago. This chapter will allow us to explore different examples of civilizations that have emerged in the past, looking at the factors that helped them to develop as well as their different achievements.

How can we find out about the past?

Before exploring examples of ancient civilizations it is worth taking the time to consider the ways in which we can find out about the past. The study of history involves the interpretation of the evidence that remains of the past. This evidence can come in many different forms; for instance, the ruins of an Ancient Roman city could provide a range of clues about the way of life for people living at that time, as well as architectural styles, systems of government, art, religion and more. Taking a more modern example, a newspaper from the time of the First World War would provide a range of information we could use to gain a better understanding of the war and how it was reported.

Historical sources are often divided into the categories of **primary** and **secondary** sources. Primary sources are typically produced at the time of an event or are artefacts from the time. Secondary sources are usually produced later than the event, and usually involve some form of account or interpretation of something that happened in the past. People who study history for a living are called historians and they are concerned with the different ways in which we can understand past societies from gathering evidence and making interpretations.

■ Table 3.1

Examples of primary sources	Examples of secondary sources
Newspapers	Books on history
Diaries	School textbooks
Photographs	Journals and academic articles
Artefacts (for example, coins, pottery, jewelry, clothing)	Biographies
Letters	Magazines
Art, music	Websites

■ ATL

Critical-thinking skills – Draw reasonable conclusions and generalizations

Consider the following primary sources and their descriptions and then copy and complete a table like the one shown.

SOURCE A

■ **Figure 3.2** A silver coin, known as a 'denarius', showing the Roman Emperor Marcus Aurelius who ruled Ancient Rome between 161CE and 180CE

DISCUSS

1 If someone from the future wanted to find out about life in the twenty-first century, what sources would you suggest they use?
2 If you created a time capsule to represent your own life, what items would you include? Think about the information each item would provide to someone in the future.

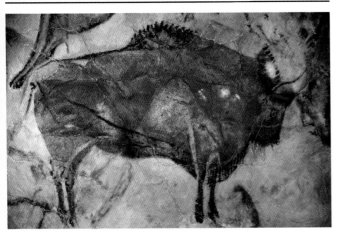

■ **Figure 3.3** Cave painting of a bison from a cave near Santander in Spain, thought to have been made during the Upper Paleolithic period of the Stone Age – somewhere between 50 000 and 10 000 years ago

■ **Figure 3.4** Thousands of these Terracotta Warriors, near Xi'an China, were buried with the Emperor Qin and are dated to around 209BCE

Source	What is going on? *What is your interpretation of the source? What claims can you make about the source?*	What makes you say that? *Provide an explanation of your point of view. Refer to details in the source or your own ideas.*
A: Coin from Ancient Rome		
B: Cave painting from prehistoric times		
C: Terracotta Warriors from Dynastic China		

DISCUSS

'It is impossible to write ancient history because we do not have enough sources and impossible to write modern history because we have far too many.'

Charles Pierre Peguy

What do you think would be the challenges of studying history if you had access to a) too few sources, or b) too many sources?

The study of history is also affected by **interpretation**. People can interpret the same events in different ways, leading to differences of opinion. These differences of opinion are sometimes called perspectives. It is a very useful skill to be able to recognize some of these differences in order to understand the perspective of the writer or historian. For example, when a war breaks out there are often different interpretations of who is to blame or why it happened. These different interpretations can be influenced by a range of factors, including the evidence that the historian has access to or perhaps his or her own personal political opinion.

When studying ancient history, there is a further challenge to finding out about the past – the availability of sources. Many of these civilizations all but disappeared many years ago and the preservation of the evidence from this time is not easy to maintain. Much of the remaining artefacts from ancient civilizations are looked after in museums around the world or have stayed in the same place in a specific location that is looked after by an organization. Some of the evidence of these past societies has been destroyed through the effects of natural disasters, conquest and wars, adding further challenges to the unlocking of their secrets.

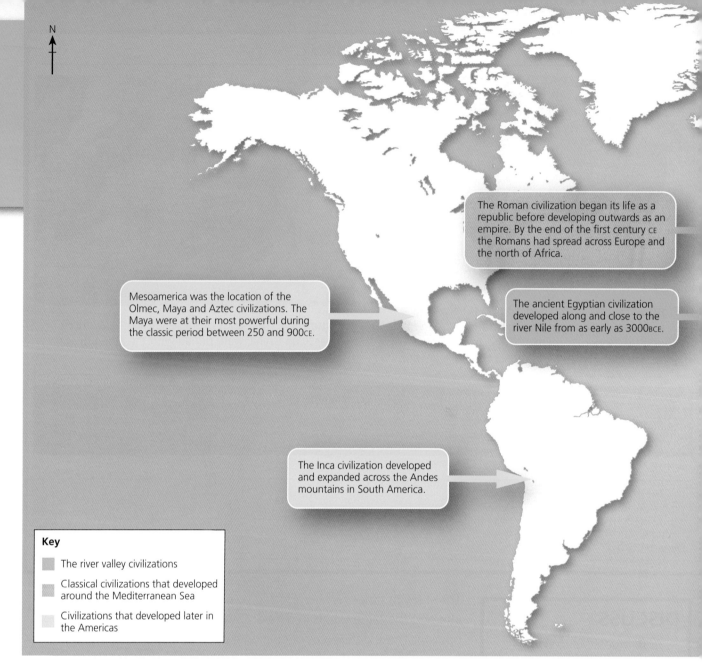

The Roman civilization began its life as a republic before developing outwards as an empire. By the end of the first century CE the Romans had spread across Europe and the north of Africa.

Mesoamerica was the location of the Olmec, Maya and Aztec civilizations. The Maya were at their most powerful during the classic period between 250 and 900CE.

The ancient Egyptian civilization developed along and close to the river Nile from as early as 3000BCE.

The Inca civilization developed and expanded across the Andes mountains in South America.

Key

- The river valley civilizations
- Classical civilizations that developed around the Mediterranean Sea
- Civilizations that developed later in the Americas

■ **Figure 3.5** Ancient civilizations

WHAT IS A CIVILIZATION?

Civilization is a term used to refer to an advanced society at a particular time period in history. Civilizations developed from earlier hunter-gatherer societies to be more centrally controlled and organized and, therefore, more complex. The main reason why this change happened was because of advances in farming techniques that allowed greater levels of production. This meant that people could focus on a wider range of other jobs. Work diversified to include builders, craft workers and religious and governmental positions.

This led to the development of power structures and the development of city states, often with impressive buildings and specific cultural and belief systems.

One problem with using the term civilization is that there are many different ways we could interpret 'advanced' society, which may be down to our individual perspective. Consequently, that can lead us to view other societies at the time as uncivilized or primitive. The term barbarian has often been used to describe non-civilized people but at times this can be misleading.

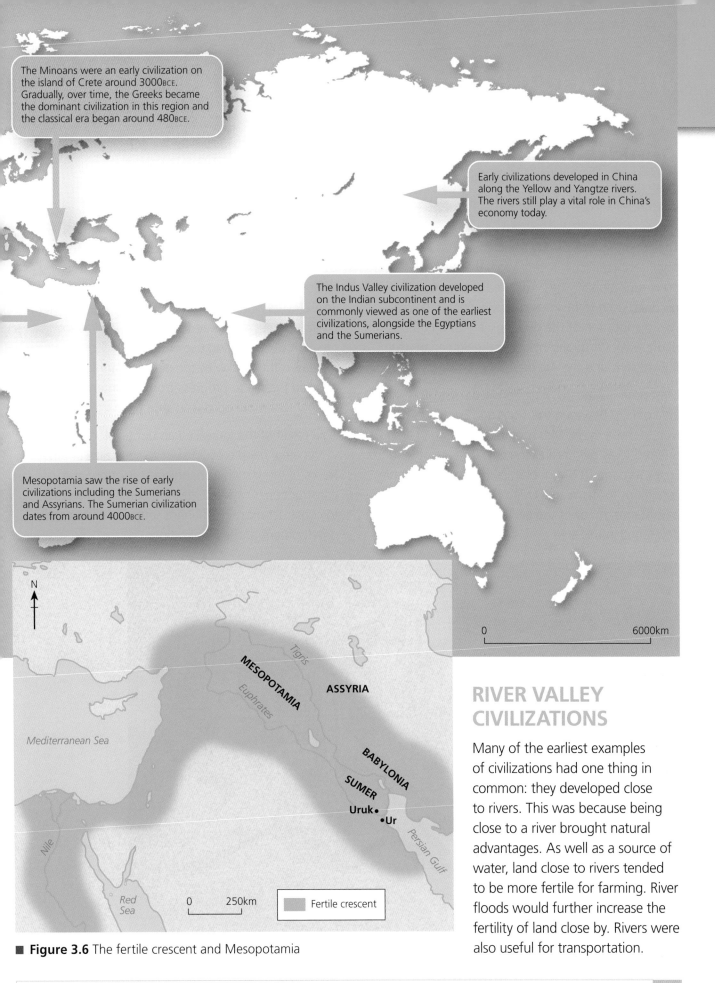

The Minoans were an early civilization on the island of Crete around 3000BCE. Gradually, over time, the Greeks became the dominant civilization in this region and the classical era began around 480BCE.

Early civilizations developed in China along the Yellow and Yangtze rivers. The rivers still play a vital role in China's economy today.

The Indus Valley civilization developed on the Indian subcontinent and is commonly viewed as one of the earliest civilizations, alongside the Egyptians and the Sumerians.

Mesopotamia saw the rise of early civilizations including the Sumerians and Assyrians. The Sumerian civilization dates from around 4000BCE.

0   6000km

N

Tigris

MESOPOTAMIA   ASSYRIA

Euphrates

Mediterranean Sea

BABYLONIA

SUMER

Uruk•
•Ur

Persian Gulf

Nile

Red
Sea

0   250km   ▢ Fertile crescent

■ **Figure 3.6** The fertile crescent and Mesopotamia

RIVER VALLEY CIVILIZATIONS

Many of the earliest examples of civilizations had one thing in common: they developed close to rivers. This was because being close to a river brought natural advantages. As well as a source of water, land close to rivers tended to be more fertile for farming. River floods would further increase the fertility of land close by. Rivers were also useful for transportation.

What were the achievements of the Sumerian civilization?

The country of Iraq in the Middle East has experienced significant conflict in recent years that has created numerous global issues. The area of land that Iraq occupies used to be known as Mesopotamia and was the location of the development of a number of ancient civilizations including the Sumerians, the Babylonians and the Assyrians.

Mesopotamia means 'between two rivers'. It was the area of land between the Tigris and Euphrates rivers. Due to these rivers, Mesopotamia was also in an area referred to as the 'fertile crescent' – an arc of land from Egypt through to Mesopotamia that had favourable conditions for farming. Owing to these natural advantages, many of the earliest human civilizations developed in this area.

HOW THE CIVILIZATION DEVELOPED

The Sumerian civilization developed towards the south of Mesopotamia and was established in the region of Sumer, between the Tigris and Euphrates rivers. These rivers aided the development of the Sumerian civilization because their flooding, as well as the creation of canals and use of irrigation techniques, increased the fertility of the land for farming. This allowed people to progress from a hunter-gatherer society to a more advanced structure.

As a result of the increased amount of food produced in the area, people could start to specialize in other forms of work such as handicrafts, pottery and construction. Consequently, the Sumerians were able to construct more permanent settlements to aid the development of their civilization.

■ **Figure 3.7** The ziggurat at Ur, an ancient Sumerian city

These settlements developed in the form of city states. Each city state was dedicated to a different god and although they were all part of Sumer, they occasionally came into conflict with each other. A central feature of the city state was the ziggurat, a pyramid structure that was said to house the specific god that the population of the city state worshipped, and the high priest would be based here. The ziggurats demonstrated the advances that the Sumerians had made in terms of architecture. The city states were usually walled. As well as having a specific god, each city state was ruled by an individual who was responsible for religious, political, military and economic control over the society.

The Sumerians, as well as being regarded as the oldest example of human civilization, were also responsible for a number of scientific and technical innovations that have subsequently influenced human history.

INNOVATIONS OF THE SUMERIANS

Writing

Sumerian writing involved the use of cuneiform. This is the use of symbols to represent different things that are communicated. The writing of the Sumerians was usually recorded on stone tablets by scribes whose job was to record the thoughts and sayings of the *ensí* (ruler) in a particular city state.

Farming

Developments in farming aided the development of the Sumerian civilization. Of particular note was the **irrigation** technique of using canals to channel the water around. A challenge faced by the Sumerians was the unpredictable flooding of the Tigris and Euphrates that often created problems for farming.

The wheel

Although disputed, many historians and archeologists claim that the Sumerians were the first to develop the wheel. It is thought that they used the wheel on chariots that were an early form of transport.

Numbers

The Sumerians also developed a number system primarily based around the number 60 (as opposed to our present system based around the number 10). This led to the development of 60 minutes in an hour and 360 degrees in a circle, which are used today.

Building

Buildings were constructed in the Sumerian city states and perhaps the best known were the ziggurats, pyramid structures with flat roofs. They were usually built with sun-dried mud bricks that were ideal for the construction of ziggurats.

Bronze

The Sumerians were also noted for their use of bronze in the creation of different tools and weaponry. This was a sign of their advanced nature as a civilization.

The Sumerian civilization was eventually overrun by other civilizations in the same area, including the Babylonians and the Assyrians. However, the Sumerians continued to influence other areas through the use of similar language, customs and technological advances.

What other civilizations flourished in Mesopotamia?

ⓘ The *Epic of Gilgamesh*

Regarded as the oldest work of literature in the world, the *Epic of Gilgamesh* is a collection of poems dating back to 2100BCE about an ancient Sumerian king, Gilgamesh. It tells the story of the king doing battle with Enkida, a wild man sent by the gods to teach Gilgamesh a lesson for repressing the people of the city state of Uruk. After the battle, Gilgamesh and Enkida become close friends and have a variety of adventures together. Enkida is later killed by the gods and Gilgamesh, traumatized by this loss, seeks to find answers to some of life's questions.

The Sumerians were not the only civilization to flourish in the region of Mesopotamia. Other examples include the Babylonians and Assyrians. You may have heard of the Babylonian Empire through references to the Hanging Gardens of Babylon, one of the seven wonders of the ancient world, and the famous ruler, King Hammurabi, who developed a law code. Hammurabi's code records 282 laws that were enacted in the region at the time, including the law 'an eye for an eye'. Many of the laws provided very harsh punishments if broken but also introduced the concept of innocent until proven guilty, an important feature of modern legal systems.

> ## REFLECTION
>
> What were some of the key achievements of the Sumerians? What else would you like to know about their civilization?

■ **Figure 3.8** Theatre students performing a modern adaptation of the *Epic of Gilgamesh* at Baghdad Fine Arts Academy

■ **Figure 3.9** Hammurabi's Code of 282 laws is inscribed on this stelae

What were the achievements of the Egyptian civilizations?

The ancient Egyptian civilizations were in existence for more than 3,000 years, occupying the same area as that of the modern nation of Egypt.

Ancient Egypt did not consist of one continuous civilization; there were a number of different kingdoms which divided this time period:
- the Old Kingdom (2649–2151BCE),
- the Middle Kingdom (2040–1630BCE) and
- the New Kingdom (1550–1070BCE).

The years between these kingdoms were known as intermediate periods.

AGRICULTURE AND IRRIGATION

Like the Sumerians, the Egyptian civilization developed due to the natural advantages of rivers, in this case the Nile. The river Nile is the longest river in the world, flowing for around 6,700km in the continent of Africa.

Back then, it provided many natural resources that helped the development of the Ancient Egyptian civilization. It provided food, a source of transportation, deposits of mud used for building materials and, most importantly, fertile soils on its banks. This fertile soil allowed for the development of the civilization as different crops could be grown in abundance to help establish more complex societies (Table 3.2).

Added to this, the Nile floods annually and this enabled wider areas of land surrounding the river to become fertile for farming. The Egyptians developed irrigation techniques to aid this process, including the diverting of water using channels.

■ **Table 3.2** Crops grown by the Ancient Egyptians and their uses

Crops grown by the Ancient Egyptians	Uses
Wheat	Bread
Barley	Beer
Flax	Rope
Papyrus	Paper and boats
Herbs	Cooking and medicine
Henna	Dye
Fruit and vegetables	Food

CITIES

The Egyptian civilizations saw the development of cities, with Memphis, Alexandria and Thebes being significant examples. These cities were ruled by pharaohs who were the political, military and religious leaders of the time.

The pharaohs were concerned with how they would fare in the afterlife so had great tombs built during their lifetime; when they were buried a vast assortment of treasures was buried with them. The most famous example of this is the tomb of Tutankhamun, which was discovered in 1922 by the archeologist Howard Carter.

Within the tomb, a variety of treasures were discovered that provided clues about the ancient Egyptian civilization. The tomb of Tutankhamun was discovered in an area of Egypt called the Valley of Kings, where many other pharaohs were buried. Despite the sensational discovery, the actual significance of Tutankhamun to the Egyptian civilization is fairly limited in comparison to other leaders.

SOURCE A

Extract from The Tomb of Tutankhamun *by Howard Carter (1923)*

'Slowly, desperately slowly it seemed to us as we watched, the remains of passage debris that encumbered the lower part of the doorway were removed, until at last we had the whole door clear before us. The decisive moment had arrived. With trembling hands I made a tiny breach in the upper left hand corner. Darkness and blank space, as far as an iron testing-rod could reach, showed that whatever lay beyond was empty, and not filled like the passage we had just cleared. Candle tests were applied as a precaution against possible foul gases, and then, widening the hole a little, I inserted the candle and peered in, Lord Carnarvon, Lady Evelyn [Lord Carnarvon's daughter] and Callender [an assistant] standing anxiously beside me to hear the verdict. At first I could see nothing, the hot air escaping from the chamber causing the candle flame to flicker, but presently, as my eyes grew accustomed to the light, details of the room within emerged slowly from the mist, strange animals, statues, and gold – everywhere the glint of gold. For the moment – an eternity it must have seemed to the others standing by – I was struck dumb with amazement, and when Lord Carnarvon, unable to stand the suspense any longer, inquired anxiously, "Can you see anything?" it was all I could do to get out the words, "Yes, wonderful things." Then widening the hole a little further, so that we both could see, we inserted an electric torch.'

SOURCE B

■ **Figure 3.10** Howard Carter excavating the sarcophagus (coffin) of Tutankhamun

ACTIVITY: Discovering Tutankhamun

■ ATL

Communication skills – Use appropriate forms of writing for different purposes and audiences

Take on the role of a member of the archeological team that unearthed the tomb of Tutankhamun using sources A–C. Write a letter to the museum that you work with to **explain** your discovery and its potential significance.

SOURCE C

Extract from 'King Tut: The Pharaoh Returns!', Smithsonian Magazine, June 2005

'Widening the opening and shining a flashlight into the room, Carter and Carnarvon saw effigies of a king, falconheaded figures, a golden throne, overturned chariots, a gilded snake, and "gold—everywhere the glint of gold." Carter later recalled that his first impression was of uncovering "the property room of an opera of a vanished civilization."

'Carter spent nearly three months photographing and clearing out the antechamber's objects alone. Then in mid-February 1923, after digging out the blocked doorway to the burial chamber, he encountered what appeared to be a solid wall of gold. This proved to be the outermost of four nested gilded wood shrines, an imposing construction—17 feet long, 11 feet wide and 9 feet high, embellished inside with scenes of winged goddesses, pharaohs and written spells—that enclosed Tutankhamun's yellow quartzite sarcophagus.'

www.smithsonianmag.com/history/king-tut-the-pharaoh-returns

■ **Figure 3.11** An archeologist at work

CONSTRUCTION

Perhaps the most iconic association with the Ancient Egyptians is that of the Great Sphinx and pyramids at Giza, close to Cairo, built during the Old Kingdom. These structures help us to understand how advanced the Ancient Egyptians were in terms of building, but it is still a mystery how the pyramids were constructed given the lack of technology to lift such heavy materials. It is thought that the pyramids were built, brick by brick, by slave labourers over many years.

WRITING

The Ancient Egyptians also demonstrated advances in communication. A system of writing called hieroglyphics was developed. Like the Sumerians, they used symbols to represent different things. The hieroglyphs were recorded by scribes on papyrus reed (papyrus comes from a plant and is a thick form of paper). Egyptologists have been able to translate these hieroglyphics thanks to the discovery of the Rosetta Stone in the late eighteenth century. This stone, produced towards the end of the civilization, presents the same information in both Ancient Egyptian hieroglyphics and Ancient Greek. Owing to the text being identical, experts have been able to translate the meanings of the hieroglyphs.

REFLECTION: The achievements of the Sumerian and Egyptian civilizations

■ ATL

Reflection skills – Consider content (What did I learn about today? What don't I yet understand? What questions do I have now?)

Think about what you have learned about the Sumerians and Ancient Egyptians and copy and complete the table below.

Civilization	What did I learn about?	What don't I yet understand?	What questions do I have now?
Sumerians			
Ancient Egyptians			

MEDICINE

The Ancient Egyptians also made some advances in the field of medicine. The practice of mummification led to a more developed understanding of human anatomy. Mummification was the process for the preparation of dead bodies before they were put into a tomb. The internal organs, apart from the heart, were removed and the body was embalmed, a process that helped with the preservation of the body.

Owing to these technical procedures, the Ancient Egyptians were able to increase their understanding of the human body. They also made connections between the river Nile and the human body. They thought that the human body was full of channels and problems occurred due to blockages, similar to the problems that would result if a channel of the river became blocked up. The Ancient Egyptians also developed a range of surgical techniques that were usually used to treat external problems. As well as this, there was also encouragement of a healthy diet, largely thanks to the range of crops, fruits and vegetables they could grow on the land surrounding the Nile.

What were the major contributions of the Ancient Greek civilization?

The **classical** era or classic antiquity was a historic time period that saw the advancement of civilizations around the Mediterranean Sea, most notably that of the Ancient Greek and Ancient Roman civilizations. These civilizations introduced a wide variety of advances that have made them significant in the development of history. The end of the classical era coincided with the end of the Roman Empire, which marked the beginning of the Dark Ages in Europe.

Ancient Greece during the classical era saw the development of mathematics, science, philosophy, medicine, the arts and politics. It is a widely held view that the Ancient Greek civilization directed the development of civilization in the West.

DEMOCRACY

The Ancient Greeks lived in and around the area occupied by modern day Greece and the civilization comprised a variety of city states of which Athens is perhaps the best known. Athens was particularly advanced politically, and it was the first place in the world to experiment with a system of democracy. Leaders of the city state were selected from a lottery of eligible citizens: men who had completed military training and who were over the age of 30. Citizens also voted in favour of or against the laws that were introduced.

The number of eligible people who could vote was not a significant amount and excluded women. Women, for the most part, had the status of second-class citizens in Ancient Greece. Despite these limitations, Athens is thought of as the birthplace of democracy and then became a model for subsequent forms of government that looked to represent the interests of the people more fairly.

PHILOSOPHY

As well as the advances in politics, the Greeks were also responsible for many of the developments in philosophy. Philosophy is the study of knowledge and it attempts to explain different ways to live life and offers plenty of opportunity for deep reflection. Famous Greek philosophers include Socrates, Plato and Aristotle, who all sought to ask questions about life and made contributions that are widely studied today.

Sparta

As mentioned before, the Ancient Greek civilization was made up of city states, with different features and rules. For example, the city state of Sparta was radically different from that of Athens. Sparta was run as a warrior state where men were judged on their ability to fight. Warriors from Sparta famously fought the Persian Empire in the Battle of Thermopylae in 480BCE. This famous battle has heightened the historical reputation of the Spartans as fearless warriors who fought to the death. Most accounts of the wars between the Greek and Persian civilizations were from the Greek historian Herodotus. Later on, Sparta went to war against Athens in the Peloponnesian war (431–404BCE)

ACTIVITY: Significant individuals of the Ancient Greek civilization

■ ATL

Information literacy skills – Access information to be informed and inform others

Choose an example of a significant individual from Ancient Greece, either from this chapter or from your own research, and create a 3–5 minute presentation about him or her. Think about covering the following information in your presentation:
- **background information about the individual**
- **work and achievements**
- **significance and lasting impact.**

Remember to include a bibliography of any sources you have used and pay attention to the quality of your written and oral presentation; it should be clear and well-organized.

◆ Assessment opportunities:

This activity can be assessed using Criterion A: Knowing and understanding (strands i and ii) and Criterion C: Communicating (strands i, ii and iii).

HERODOTUS – Regarded as the 'father of history', Herodotus was a historian who recorded many accounts during his life. Most famous were his accounts of the Persian wars fought between the Persian and Greek civilizations. His style of writing often relied on entertaining stories about events.

■ **Figure 3.12a** Herodotus wrote his Histories in the 450s BC

PYTHAGORAS – A very familiar name in mathematics, Pythagoras was a mathematician and philosopher who is associated with the theorem that the square of the hypotenuse is equal to the sum of the squares of the other two sides of a right-angled triangle. Pythagoras may be misattributed with this discovery.

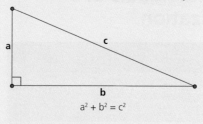

$$a^2 + b^2 = c^2$$

■ **Figure 3.12b** Pythagoras's theorem

ARCHIMEDES – A scientist and mathematician, Archimedes made many discoveries during his lifetime in the field of mathematics, science and engineering. A famous example is the Archimedes screw, a hand-operated machine that is used to transport water from a low level to an elevated level. This had particular benefits in agriculture, for irrigation purposes.

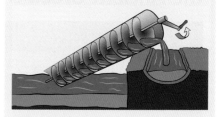

■ **Figure 3.12c** Archimedes's screw

HOMER – Author of the *Iliad* and the *Odyssey*. Homer's epic poems are classical works of literature. The *Iliad* is set during the Trojan wars and tells the story of Achilles, an immortal warrior, who had one weakness: his heel. The *Odyssey* is about the ten-year journey of the central character, Odysseus, to return home after the Trojan wars. During this time he does battle with the gods who feature prominently in Homer's work. The works of Homer mark the beginning of the classical era.

■ **Figure 3.12d** Homer was considered to be the greatest epic poet

HIPPOCRATES – Often regarded as the father of modern medicine, Hippocrates was influential in his search for natural explanations for medical conditions. In the past, many medical conditions had been explained through the gods. The Hippocratic Oath dates from this time and is a commitment by medical practitioners to maintain ethical standards of protecting human life. Hippocrates's influence can still be seen to this day.

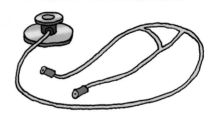

■ **Figure 3.12e** Hippocrates's ideas still influence doctors today

ALEXANDER THE GREAT – A political and military leader who was taught by Aristotle, Alexander the Great was responsible for the expansion of the Greek Empire across a wide swathe of territory stretching from Egypt to India. His military tactics have been studied ever since.

■ **Figure 3.12f** Alexander conquered the Persian Empire at the age of 25

EUCLID – A mathematician whose contribution to the development of geometry is significant. His book *Elements of Geometry* had a significant impact on the development of mathematics.

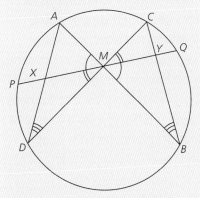

■ **Figure 3.12i** An example of Euclidian geometry

SOCRATES – A philosopher whose influence is still relevant today. His ideas have influenced the development of political and legal systems in history. In addition, the 'Socratic Method', a critical-thinking approach to discussing issues continues to be a widely used method of reaching conclusions and, moreover, asking questions.

■ **Figure 3.12g** Socrates taught his students to question everything

PLATO – A student of Socrates, and resident of the city state of Athens, Plato's contribution to philosophy is significant; he advocated the importance of thinking more carefully about our own lives. Plato also reflected on the ideal society in the *Republic*, where rulers were enlightened individuals who made decisions for the good of all people.

■ **Figure 3.12j** Plato's *Republic* is one of the most influential works of political theory

ARISTOTLE – A philosopher, scientist and teacher, he wrote many books and studied with Plato. He founded a school called the Lyceum. His contributions to understanding happiness often focused on the ways that people could lead a good life, which often involved finding a balance in their different behaviours.

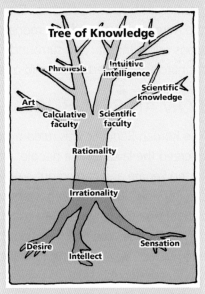

■ **Figure 3.12h** Aristotle's Tree of Knowledge

How did the Roman civilization change over time?

The settlement of Rome began long before the Romans became a powerful civilization. The natural advantages of the city included its proximity to the river Tiber, fertile land for farming and an elevated position to help with defence. The early civilization of the Romans developed as a monarchy with different kings ruling the city and surrounding area. In 509CE the monarchy was overthrown and a republic was set up.

ROMAN REPUBLIC

The Roman Republic was ruled by a senate that decreed the laws for the people. Officials were elected to the Senate and carried out a variety of roles to run the Republic. The most important position within the Senate was the consul. There could only ever be two consuls at one time and they had the power to veto each other. The consuls could make major decisions for the whole Republic such as deciding to go to war or the passing of new laws.

Society was divided into three main classes:
- The patrician class was the aristocracy of the time, landowners who held the greatest levels of wealth and, consequently, power.
- The plebians included farmers, builders and people who worked in various crafts. Over time, they gradually gained more political power and the ability to vote for members of the Senate.
- The slaves had limited rights and were considered the property of other people.

ⓘ **Republic** – A system of government where the state is ruled by elected representatives

Empire – A variety of places ruled by a single, supreme authority

ROMAN EMPIRE

The Roman Republic was gradually replaced with the Roman Empire. This was a shift in the political structure, which led to more power being concentrated in the hands of an individual ruler, the emperor. This process began under Julius Caesar and continued under his heir, Octavian, who took on the name Augustus for his rule from 27BCE. As an empire, Rome expanded its influence across what we know today as Europe and North Africa.

The Romans connected their empire together with roads, often stretching for hundreds of miles. This encouraged the development of trade and allowed for better communication between distant places.

They developed architectural designs including the aqueduct, used to transport water over long distances, and amphitheatres for different forms of entertainment. They also developed various public health facilities in their towns and cities, including bathhouses. The Romans pioneered the development of the arch in building design and bridge design; the arch was used to support heavy weights. The Romans also valued entertainment and there were a variety of games and contests that were popular with people throughout the Roman Empire.

Military strength was another feature of the Roman civilization. The Romans developed organized structures for running the army and utilized new technology in their weaponry. The Roman army was able to expand the territory of the Roman Empire and defend it from attack.

However, the size of the Roman Empire proved increasingly difficult to control and ultimately was a major factor behind its decline. The pressures of trying to keep the empire together proved too great and it was eventually split into the Eastern and Western Roman Empire. The Eastern half went on to become the Byzantine Empire and lasted for around 1,000 years, while the Western half declined and fell from power as it was increasingly attacked by rival groups in Europe.

ℹ️ Romulus and Remus

The founding myth of Rome is the story of Romulus and Remus, twin brothers who were the sons of the Roman God of War, Mars. They were abandoned and left in a basket in the river Tiber but were found by a wolf who raised them as her own. Eventually, they were rescued by a shepherd who took them home and raised them as his own children. Their identity was eventually realized and they set about establishing a city in their area. The two brothers disagreed on the location, and Remus was killed by Romulus as their disagreement intensified. Romulus went on to found the city of Rome and became the first king. There are a number of variations of the story.

■ **Figure 3.13** A Roman soldier

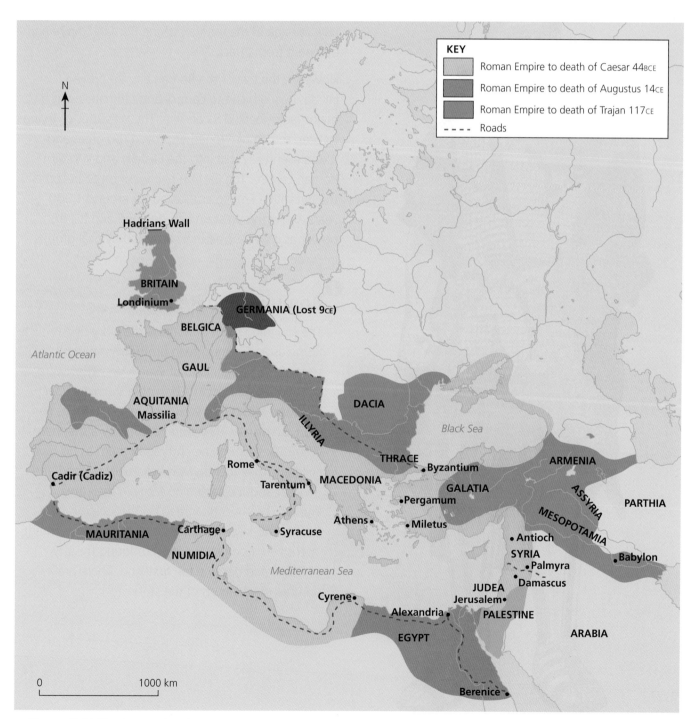

■ **Figure 3.14** The Roman Empire, 44BCE–117CE

What has been the legacy of the Roman civilization?

Roman numerals

Used as a numbering system by the Romans, we still use this system in various ways today. For example, monarchs have adopted Roman numerals to indicate their position in history (for example, King George V), and many watch faces feature Roman numerals instead of numbers for aesthetic purposes.

Julian calendar

Created under Julius Caesar, the Julian calendar consisted of 365 days per year and 12 months. However, because of issues with leap years (which have 366 days), this system was modified to the Gregorian calendar in the sixteenth century, which is now the dominant way of measuring days, months and years in the world. The Julian calendar was an important step towards developing the calendar we use today.

Language

Latin was the major linguistic contribution of the Roman world. This had an important impact on the development of many languages including French, Spanish and Portuguese.

Public health

The Romans were concerned about health and how they could provide for the people living under the rule of the Empire. Many public health facilities were established including bathhouses, aqueducts and drainage systems. People were also encouraged to adopt a healthy lifestyle through exercise and good food.

Law and politics

The democratic features of the Senate have influenced the development of democracy in later centuries. Roman law was written down in the form of the Law of the 12 Tables, influencing subsequent legal systems.

Religion

The adoption of Christianity by the Roman Empire in the form of the Roman Catholic Church was an important development in the history of Christianity. The head of the Catholic Church, the Pope, is based in the Vatican, an independent state within the city of Rome.

SOURCE A

Extract about gladiators from The Roman Empire, *a PBS television series*

'Successful gladiators were the movie stars of the first century – so famous that free men queued to take their chances in the arena. Bloody, brutal but popular, gladiatorial contests are often seen as the dark side of Roman civilization.

'Given they belonged to such a civilized and sophisticated society, the Romans' deep attraction to extreme violence remains surprising and strange. Historians have struggled to explain how a country that civilized so much of the world could be so keen on watching men and women fight to the death.'

SOURCE B

Extract from Seneca's Moral Epistles, *written around 60CE*

'The gladiators have nothing to protect them: their bodies are utterly open to every blow: every thrust finds its mark... Most people prefer this kind of thing to all other matches... The sword is not checked by helmet or shield. What good is armour? What good is swordsmanship? All these things only put off death a little. In the morning men are matched with lions and bears, at noon with their spectators... death is the fighters' only exit.'

■ **Figure 3.15** The Coliseum in Rome, the location of many gladiator matches

■ **Figure 3.16** Painting by Jean-Leon Gerome in 1872 called 'Pollice Verso' (with a turned thumb)

SEE–THINK–WONDER

Study Source D, 'Pollice Verso', and then complete the following routine in groups.

What do you see?

What do you think about that?

What does it make you wonder?

SOURCE E

Explanation about the role of the games from the Ancient History Encyclopedia website

'Roman gladiator games were an opportunity for Emperors and rich aristocrats to display their wealth to the populace, to commemorate military victories, mark visits from important officials, celebrate birthdays or simply to distract the populace from the political and economic problems of the day. The appeal to the public of the games was as bloody entertainment and the fascination which came from contests which were literally a matter of life and death. Hugely popular events were held in massive arenas throughout the Empire, with the Colosseum (or Flavian Amphitheatre) the biggest of them all. Thirty, forty or even fifty thousand spectators from all sections of Roman society flocked to be entertained by gory spectacles where wild and exotic animals were hunted, prisoners were executed, religious martyrs were thrown to the lions and the stars of the show, symbols of the Roman virtues of honour and courage, the gladiators, employed all their martial skills in a kill or be killed contest.'

www.ancient.eu

ACTIVITY: Roman entertainment

■ ATL

- Critical-thinking skills – Draw reasonable conclusions and generalizations

Study the sources on pages 67–69 and answer the following questions.

1 Copy and complete the table.

Source	What is the origin of the source?	What is the purpose of the source?	What does the source suggest about the Roman games?
A			
B			
C			
D			
E			

2 Does the existence of the Roman games suggest that the Romans were not a civilized society?
  Use all the sources and your own ideas to **discuss** this question. Think about the perspectives of different groups within Roman society such as the emperor, the patricians, the plebians, slaves, the young, the old. What might they say about the Roman games?

◆ Assessment opportunities:

This activity can be assessed using Criterion D: Thinking critically (strands ii, iii and iv).

What were the features of the Maya and Inca civilizations?

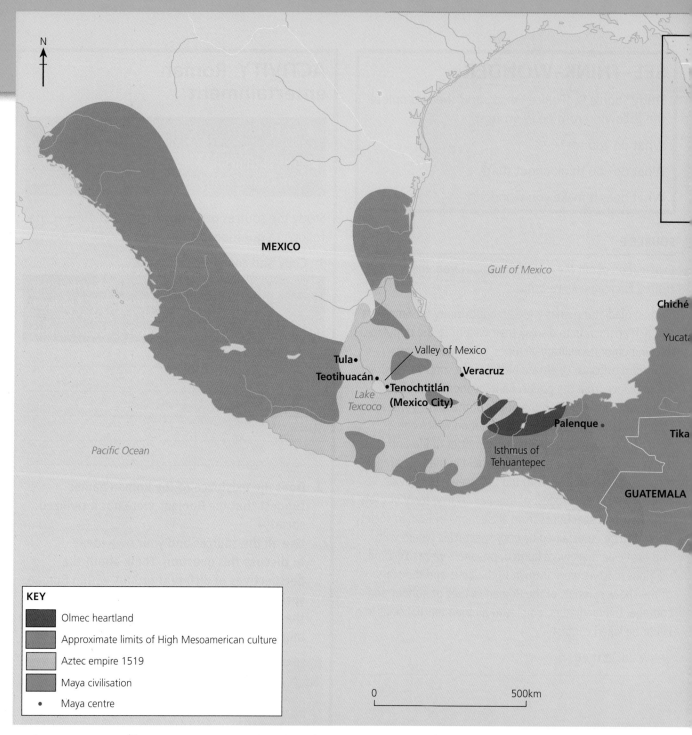

N

MEXICO

Gulf of Mexico

Chiché

Yucata

Valley of Mexico

Tula •
Teotihuacán •
• Veracruz
• Tenochtitlán
(Mexico City)

Lake
Texcoco

Pacific Ocean

Palenque •

Tika

Isthmus of
Tehuantepec

GUATEMALA

KEY

Olmec heartland

Approximate limits of High Mesoamerican culture

Aztec empire 1519

Maya civilisation

• Maya centre

0   500km

■ **Figure 3.17** Map of Mesoamerica

▼ Links to: Mathematics

The Maya developed complex systems of measuring time with a great deal of accuracy. They were advanced mathematically.
Explore the different ways that the Maya used mathematics.

Caribbean Sea

m

NDURAS

NICARAGUA

COSTA RICA

PANAMA

THE MAYA

The civilization of the Maya people emerged in Mesoamerica. Mesoamerica is the area of central America between Panama and the north of Mexico. A number of civilizations emerged in this region due to a variety of favourable conditions that helped the development of cities and settlements. Other civilizations include the Olmec, who preceded the Maya and greatly influenced them, and the better-known Aztec civilization who emerged slightly later in Mexico.

The Mesoamerican civilizations developed in complete isolation from other civilizations in the world such as those in Mesopotamia, Egypt and the Mediterranean. The climate and topography of Mesoamerica could not be more different from these areas. While Mesopotamia and Egypt were largely desert, Mesoamerica is mostly rainforest – hot and wet all year round with dense vegetation.

Like the Egyptians, Greeks and Sumerians, the Maya civilization also developed in the form of city states. These city states were structured and had religious leaders. They sometimes fought with each other. Within the city states, the Maya built pyramids, palaces, housing and courts for ball games. Famous ruins of Mayan city states can be found at Tikal in Guatemala and Chichén Itzá in the south of Mexico.

The Maya civilizations were at their peak between 300–800ce. During this time they were able to build on many of their achievements and expand their influence in Mesoamerica. One of the achievements of the Maya is the use of writing. Using a similar system to the Egyptians, the Maya used hieroglyphics to communicate written information. This was recorded on paper that was made from different materials available in the locality, such as tree bark.

The Maya were also advanced in their use of numbers and developed the use of zero as a number. This was an advanced concept as it allowed far more complexity of understanding of numbers and mathematics. The Mayan calendar was 260 days per year and they developed ideas in the field of astronomy. Another, more grizzly, feature of Maya society and culture was the use of human sacrifice that was associated with their beliefs. Although not a regular occurrence, human sacrifice influenced the Aztecs who made more widespread use of this ritual. After 800ce the Mayan civilization slowly went into decline, but the reasons for this are debated.

THE INCA

In the early twentieth century, US explorer Hiram Bingham wrote a book called *The Lost City of the Incas*. This was a book about his recent adventures in Peru where he had rediscovered the ruins of the Inca city Machu Picchu. Machu Picchu is now viewed as one of the modern wonders of the world. The existence of a small city so high in the Andes mountains was a strong indication of how advanced the Inca were.

The civilization of the Inca developed in South America, primarily in the Andes that run the length of the continent. The Inca civilization really began with the establishment of the city of Cuzco. Cuzco became the centre of the Inca Empire, through which the different power structures and the spread of their influence could be organized. The Inca are an example of a relatively recent civilization as the city of Cuzco was founded around 1200CE. Compare that to the Ancient Egyptians or Sumerians who were setting up their city states well before 2000BCE.

Over time, the Inca became a very powerful empire in South America and their influence spread from Peru to Ecuador, Bolivia, Chile and as far south as Argentina. Their territory was primarily mountainous and they did not spread much into the Amazon rainforest that takes up huge amounts of land in South America. They made use of the mountains through the development of extensive roads and paths built with stone. They were able to farm the land in the Andes through the use of terraces, which were used to farm a variety of crops. Like other civilizations, the Inca used irrigation techniques to help the growth of farming. The Inca did not develop the use of either the wheel or writing. For communication they used quipus, a system of knotting rope to communicate information. The size and type of

■ **Figure 3.18** Map of the Inca Empire

knot would indicate what was being said. Knots could be used to communicate numbers, which helped with the running of their tax system.

The Inca were organized as a hierarchy to distribute power. Families were organized into Ayllus – these were groups of families who worked together, usually in farming. There was an overall emperor or monarch of the Inca called the Sapa Inca – this individual held the greatest power over the civilization and lived in great wealth. One notable achievement in terms of organization and structures of power was the use of an extensive and well-structured tax system across the empire that used resources such as food and metals as a form of payment.

The arrival of the Spanish in the sixteenth century signalled the end of Inca dominance in the region. The Europeans brought a number of diseases that the Inca had not before been exposed to. Many Inca were killed; in particular, smallpox had a devastating impact on the indigenous people of the Americas. The Spanish went on to dominate South America politically from that point onwards. The Inca language and culture is still prevalent today, especially in Peru, where sites like Machu Picchu and Cuzco are visited by many tourists every year to experience some degree of the Inca civilization.

■ **Figure 3.19** Machu Picchu in Peru

SOURCE A

Extract from Chronicles of the Incas, 1540 *by Pedro de Cieza de Léon. Many of the written sources about the Inca are by Spanish explorers who wrote down their encounters with the Inca civilization*

'At the beginning of the new year the rulers of each village came to Cuzco, bringing their quipus, which told how many births there had been during the year, and how many deaths. In this way the Inca and the governors knew which of the Indians were poor, the women who had been widowed, whether they were able to pay their taxes, and how many men they could count on in the event of war, and many other things they considered highly important. The Incas took care to see that justice was meted [given] out, so much so that nobody ventured to commit a felony or theft.'

DISCUSS

As the Inca did not develop a system of writing, what challenges would face a historian studying their civilization? What other approaches could be used?

The debatable question for this chapter is '**Can we ever know the past?**'. From the examples that have been examined, can you think of some responses to this question?

SUMMATIVE ASSESSMENT TASK: What factors led to the emergence and achievements of different civilizations?

Your task is to **identify** and **explain** the factors that have led to the emergence and achievements of different civilizations in the past.

For this task you need to write a 500–800 word report that **explores** the factors (or reasons) why different civilizations in the past were established and what they achieved. You should try to **explore** three different factors within your answer.

Table 3.3 provides some suitable examples that you could choose to write about.

■ **Table 3.3**

Natural features and climate	Political structures and law	Individuals	Beliefs
Force	Innovation	Communication	Luck, circumstance

For example, if you were writing about individuals, the leadership of Alexander the Great would be a relevant example for the expansion of the Greek civilization.

Alternatively, if you were looking at natural features and climate, the natural advantages of the river valley for civilizations in Mesopotamia and Egypt would be relevant.

Your report should be written with a clear structure, using paragraphs and supporting your ideas with relevant evidence.

The command terms for this task are highlighted below.

Identify – Provide an answer from a number of possibilities. Recognize and state briefly a distinguishing fact or feature.

Explain – Give a detailed account including reasons or causes.

Definitions from IB MYP Individuals and societies guide, *2014*

Using evidence to support your arguments

When you are given the task of producing a piece of writing or an essay it is important to use evidence effectively to support your arguments. Evidence could be specific facts that you have found in your research, it could be a quotation from an individual on the topic you are researching, or it could be some statistical information. Try to structure your written work so that the main argument(s) that you are delivering are supported by relevant evidence to improve the overall quality of your work.

Reflection

In this chapter we have reflected on the importance of using historical sources to find out about past societies. We have explored a range of past civilizations that have been significant in world history with many advances that shape our understanding of the world today.

Use this table to reflect on your own learning in this chapter		
Questions we asked	Answers we found	Any further questions now?
Factual What were the achievements of the Sumerian and Egyptian civilizations? What were the major contributions of the Greek civilization? How did the Roman civilization change over time? What has been the legacy of the Roman civilization? What were the features of the Maya and Inca civilizations?		
Conceptual How can we find out about the past? What is a civilization? What factors led to the emergence and achievements of different civilizations?		
Debatable It possible to ever know the past?		

Approaches to learning you used in this chapter	Description – what new skills did you learn?	How well did you master the skills?			
		Novice	Learner	Practitioner	Expert
Communication skills					
Creative-thinking skills					
Critical-thinking skills					
Information literacy skills					
Reflection skills					

Learner profile attribute(s)	Reflect on the importance of being an inquirer for your learning in this chapter.
Inquirer	

4 Where do we live?

○ Settlements develop and **change** due to a variety of **processes** and their **sustainability** allows them to function successfully, affecting the **identity of that location**.

■ **Figure 4.1a** A village in Greenland

┌─○ IN THIS CHAPTER, WE WILL …

- **Find out** about the different reasons why settlements develop and how they change over time.
- **Explore** examples of settlements and the challenges and opportunities facing them.
- **Take action** by looking at ways that settlements can become more sustainable for the future.

CONSIDER THESE QUESTIONS:

Factual: What are the different types of settlement? What makes a good location for a settlement? What is meant by urbanization? Why are some settlements abandoned?

Conceptual: How do settlements change over time? How can settlements be more sustainable?

Debatable: Are cities the future?

Now **share and compare** your thoughts and ideas with your partner, or with the whole class.

■ These Approaches to Learning (ATL) skills will be useful …

- Communication skills
- Creative-thinking skills
- Critical-thinking skills
- Information literacy skills

● We will reflect on this learner profile attribute …

Communicator – providing opportunities to communicate our understanding of concepts in different ways.

◆ Assessment opportunities in this chapter:

- ◆ Criterion B: Investigating
- ◆ Criterion C: Communicating
- ◆ Criterion D: Thinking critically

■ **Figure 4.1b** A yurt with a satellite dish in Mongolia

■ **Figure 4.1c** Aerial view of Dhaka, the capital of Bangladesh

■ **Figure 4.1d** Rooftops of houses in Bath, England

ACTIVITY: Types of settlement

ATL

■ Critical-thinking skills – Draw reasonable conclusions and generalizations

1 Match the following descriptions to the pictures (Figures 4.1a–d).

   a I live a nomadic lifestyle and experience open countryside where I live. We often have to move location. My work involves herding horses, goats and sheep.

   b I live in a busy city. The traffic on the roads is often very congested.

   c I live in a small historic city that has varied types of architecture from different time periods.

   d My family and I live in a small remote village that is very isolated. We make our living through fishing.

2 What do you think it would be like to live in each of the different settlements? What do the pictures suggest about the differences that exist in the world concerning where and how people live? Can you think of advantages and disadvantages of each of the locations?

KEY WORDS

function	situation
city	sustainability

An important development in the history of human civilizations is the establishment of different **settlements** where people live. As we saw in Chapter 3, societies often originally settled in certain locations owing to their natural advantages. The change from hunter-gatherer societies to farming societies was the key factor that led to the development of early permanent settlements in the world.

Today, there is a huge variety of settlements that provide an important backdrop to people's lives. From the remote fishing villages of Greenland to the bustling streets of Dhaka, settlements provide people with a sense of home. In the twenty-first century it is predicted that the number of people living in cities will continue to rise. We will explore the implications of this in this chapter as well as exploring different types of settlements and how they change over time.

What are the different types of settlement?

To define the term 'settlements', they are simply places where people set up homes to live. Settlements vary in size ranging from communities of only a handful of people through to major cities where millions live and coexist with each other. Some settlements can be temporary (for example, nomadic settlements) and will change location many times while others have existed in the same location for hundreds of years.

■ **Figure 4.2** What type of settlement is this?

THINK–PAIR–SHARE

What examples of temporary settlement can you think of? What type of home is pictured in Figure 4.2? Why might some people choose to live this type of lifestyle?

ACTIVITY: Locating different types of settlements

■ ATL

Information literacy skills – Access information to be informed and inform others

1 On a computer, go to 'Google Maps' and find your local area. Using both the satellite imagery and the political maps, try to find examples of the following in your area:
   a isolated dwelling
   b dispersed settlement
   c linear settlement
   d nucleated settlement
   e town
   f village
   g city.

2 Find examples of settlements in your local area or further afield that have the following functions:
   a tourism
   b farming
   c commercial
   d industrial.

3 Find a satellite image of a settlement of your choice; this could be in a different country. **Annotate** the image with different features that you can see. Share your ideas with the class when you have done this. Suitable examples include Dubai, Cape Town, New York, Rio de Janeiro.

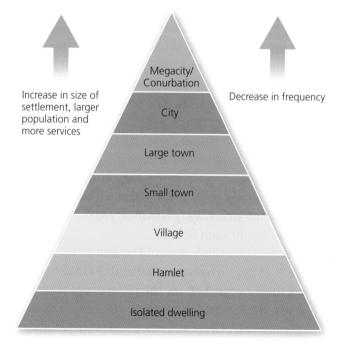

Increase in size of settlement, larger population and more services

Decrease in frequency

Megacity/Conurbation
City
Large town
Small town
Village
Hamlet
Isolated dwelling

■ **Figure 4.3** Settlement hierarchy

SETTLEMENT HIERARCHY

The varying sizes of settlement can be sorted into a settlement hierarchy, as shown in Figure 4.3.

Isolated dwelling

Usually a single house or a series of buildings that exist in isolation, this type of settlement is mostly constructed through personal choice or necessity. For instance, an individual or family may choose to build a house in an isolated location to have more space in which to live. Other isolated dwellings may be connected to a farm or an industry which requires a lot of space. These types of settlements are typically in **rural** areas.

Hamlet

Not to be confused with the play by Shakespeare, a hamlet is also the name for a very small settlement, which usually consists of a small number of houses. Hamlets do not usually have facilities such as shops. Definitions of hamlet vary depending on the country they are in but a typical population size would be about 100 inhabitants. Like isolated dwellings, they are usually located in rural areas.

Village

A village is a small settlement with quite a few houses and often there are facilities such as shops or religious buildings. The size of villages varies considerably and the larger-sized villages tend to have more of a range of facilities such as several shops, a park and religious building. Villages are usually in rural settings but sometimes they can be on the edge of **urban** areas. In addition, urban areas can develop around villages.

Town

Towns often have thousands of residents and are larger settlements. Towns are typically self-contained in terms of facilities and would usually have a high street with a range of shops and other facilities. Towns often have a civic centre for government administration as well as emergency services such as police and paramedics. Towns sometimes have a railway station that connects to other towns and cities, and bus routes in and around the town itself. A typical population size would be around 50,000–200,000 inhabitants. Towns are examples of urban settlements.

City

Cities are large settlements. Cities are usually divided into different districts, many of which have their own distinct features and facilities. Cities usually have efficient transport systems to move people around, including underground train networks. Cities are often centres of culture with art galleries, museums and other landmarks drawing people to visit them. Cities are urban in nature but can contain green spaces, such as parks, within them for recreation. Larger cities are sometimes described as **conurbations** – referring to a large urban area that sees a merging together of more than one city or with surrounding towns.

Megacity

These are the largest examples of human settlement. Megacities are cities with more than 10 million people living there. The number of megacities in the world has increased in recent years as more and more people live in cities. Megacities can sometimes be formed by the merging of different urban areas to make the city larger. An example of a megacity, the largest in the world, is Tokyo, in Japan, which has around 37 million residents in the conurbation. Megacities are at risk of experiencing overpopulation problems if not run effectively.

> ## THINK–PAIR–SHARE
> Think about where you live. What type of settlement do you live in?

SETTLEMENT FUNCTION

As well as varying in size, settlements also vary according to their **function**; this is the overall purpose of the settlement. For example, some settlements develop as ports owing to their proximity to the sea, whereas other settlements may develop as industrial centres with factories and lower-cost housing for workers. Settlements can also be linked together. For instance, a city is usually surrounded by towns and villages that have transport links to the city. This linking is described as a **sphere of influence** – the city would influence the development of nearby towns and villages often due to economic opportunities. For example, cities often provide locations for a variety of jobs while the surrounding settlements have more of a residential function. Other examples include tourism, cultural and commercial functions. Most settlements have more than one function.

DISCUSS

How might the function of a settlement define the experience of living there?

Viewed on a map, settlements can occur in different patterns. Three examples of this are **nucleated**, **dispersed** and **linear** settlement patterns.

- **Nucleated** settlements have a centre point and develop from the middle outwards. For instance, they may develop around the intersection of two major roads, a market or a religious building and then grow outwards from there.
- **Dispersed** settlements involve a number of buildings that are not that close to each other but are within the same locality. They tend to be located in rural areas and fit into the definition of isolated dwellings, hamlets and small villages.
- **Linear** settlements usually develop along an established route; this includes roads, railways and waterways. Therefore, a linear settlement might grow along a major road as this provides a valuable connection to other places to help the settlement to thrive.

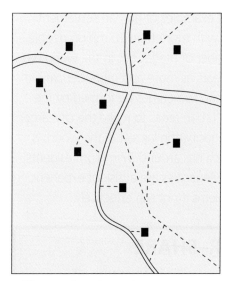

a Dispersed settlement

b Linear settlement

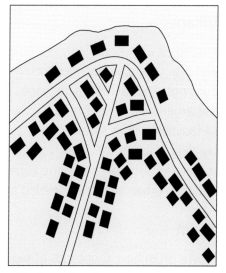

c Nucleated settlement

■ **Figure 4.4** Types of settlement pattern

What makes a good location for a settlement?

Sites for settlement are chosen according to a number of different factors, many of which are dependent on the time at which the settlement began. The site of a settlement refers to its specific location; the **situation** of a settlement refers to its position relative to nearby physical and human features. The factors influencing the development of different settlements vary but historically there have been a few common factors that have indicated whether or not a settlement will be successful.

DISCUSS

Which of the location factors listed do you think are still relevant today? Why might the factors influencing the choice of location for a settlement change over time?

- **Access to water** – The ability to access water is extremely important to the development of different settlements as they can use the water for drinking, cleaning and, if viable, a waterway for trade with other settlements.
- **Land quality** – The quality of land is important; for instance, a marsh or swamp can be problematic for settlement as it can be unhygienic and the land may not be stable enough. Flat land is often useful for establishing a settlement as it is easier to build on flat land.
- **Defence** – Depending on the time that a settlement is established, defence can be an important consideration. Some settlements can be easier to defend from attack if in a higher location or next to the coast.
- **Aspect/shelter** – Aspect refers to the positioning of a settlement: locations with a good aspect can enjoy more moderate climates, which help settlements to develop. Shelter refers to protection for the settlement: a settlement at the foot of a mountain may be protected from the weather.
- **Natural resources** – Availability of natural resources is an important consideration; for instance, access to supplies of wood and stone helps with the building and development of the settlement. Being close to a lake or the sea can provide a plentiful supply of fish for eating.
- **Attractiveness of the area** – Another consideration is the look and feel of the location. Many settlements are established because the area is desirable. Locations with great views and natural scenery have often been chosen for this exact reason.
- **Function** – A final consideration when choosing the location for a settlement is if it is to fulfil a particular function. For instance, a farming settlement needs access to fertile land for farming, a fishing settlement needs to be near the coast or a lake, and a mining town needs convenient access to the mines. Some settlements are established as satellite towns; this means that they are set to have excellent transport links to a larger city.

ACTIVITY: What makes a good location for a settlement?

Critical-thinking skills – Draw reasonable conclusions and generalizations

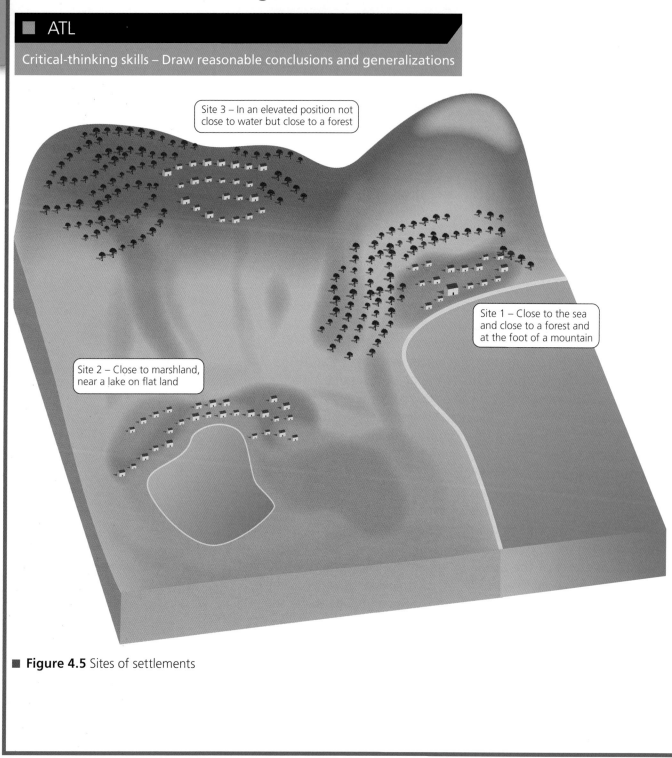

Site 3 – In an elevated position not close to water but close to a forest

Site 1 – Close to the sea and close to a forest and at the foot of a mountain

Site 2 – Close to marshland, near a lake on flat land

■ **Figure 4.5** Sites of settlements

1 Study Figure 4.5 and copy and complete the table to consider the **natural** advantages and disadvantages of each location for settlement.

Site	Advantages	Disadvantages
1		
2		
3		

2 Read through the descriptions of three different settlements and the three different identity cards (Figure 4.6). Write down who you think is most suited to each settlement and why. Once you have done this, share your ideas with a partner.

- Settlement 1 – A small city located close to the coast. It has an excellent transport system and good links with nearby towns and villages. The city has some facilities for people but is criticized for its lack of choice. The city recently won an award for its environmental policies, which include a bike rental scheme. The city has lots of parks and its residents enjoy living near the coast.

- Settlement 2 – A remote village approximately a three-hour drive from the nearest city. Set in an outstanding area of countryside, the village population includes people mainly working in rural industries, such as farming and fishing. The village is close to the coastline and there are excellent opportunities for outdoor sports. As the population is quite small, around 700 people, it is a quiet place to live.

- Settlement 3 – A major city of more than 5 million people. This city is busy and congested but has a wide variety of facilities to suit all interests. The city is a major financial centre and provides a wide range of high-paying jobs. The city has been criticized for its poor environmental policies, but applauded for its decent transportation system that enables people to keep moving around.

Name	Sidney
Age	29
Occupation	Lawyer
Status	Single
Interests	Visiting art galleries and eating out in restaurants

Name	Janice
Age	52
Occupation	Teacher
Status	Married with two teenage children
Interests	Sailing, gardening

Name	Erik
Age	36
Occupation	Web designer
Status	Married with no children
Interests	Sustainability, community projects

■ **Figure 4.6** Identity cards

◆ Assessment opportunities:

In this activity you have practised skills that can be assessed using Criterion C: Communicating.

How do settlements change over time?

All settlements change in different ways over time. Some will grow in size while others may reduce and see a drop in their population. Settlements can be affected by natural disasters, wars, new technologies, outbreaks of disease and political changes in the running of government. Consider the following three case studies of different cities to explore examples of change over time.

■ **Figure 4.7** Hong Kong in 1910 (*left*), 1972 (*top*) and 2014 (*right*)

Individuals & Societies for the IB MYP 1: by Concept

CASE STUDY 1 – HONG KONG, SAR CHINA

Hong Kong, the 'fragrant harbour', is located to the south of mainland China and is a Special Administrative Region (SAR) of the Peoples' Republic of China. Hong Kong's population is approximately 7 million and some of the most densely populated areas in the world are within the city.

Hong Kong's history provides an insight into how the city has developed and changed over time. Hong Kong originally developed as a settlement where the primary function was fishing, given its proximity to the South China Sea. Hong Kong's role changed significantly after Britain took control of Hong Kong Island after defeating China in the opium war in 1842.

Hong Kong Island after this point was governed by the British. Britain expanded its control to include Kowloon and finally the New Territories in the north of the region by the end of the nineteenth century. Hong Kong developed under British rule to utilize its geographic advantage of having a natural deep-sea port. It became a major trading hub and this had a subsequent impact on the city. Hong Kong has also developed as a major financial centre.

■ **Figure 4.8** A traditional junk boat floating in Hong Kong harbour

The city has some of the highest concentrations of population density on the planet. This has created a number of issues with housing, but at the same time large areas of land have been protected from urban development and designated as a country park.

Hong Kong was handed over from the UK to the People's Republic of China in 1997 but it has a system of government different from the rest of China due to the fact that it is a Special Administrative Region, giving it more economic and political freedom. Hong Kong has experienced challenges in recent years including a serious outbreak of the disease SARS in 2003 and a series of political protests dubbed the 'Umbrella Revolution' in 2014.

SEE–THINK–WONDER

Look at the pictures of Hong Kong in 1910, 1972 and 2014 (Figure 4.7), then **list** of the changes that you can see over time. **Discuss** the different ways that these changes might affect Hong Kong.

CASE STUDY 2 – LONDON, UK

London, the capital of the UK, has been around as a settlement for hundreds of years. Settlement in London dates back to the Roman era, with the river Thames flowing through it as a defining feature from its earliest days. The city has constantly changed over the years as can be seen in the wide variety of distinct architectural styles present in the city skyline.

London has frequently been struck by disaster including outbreaks of bubonic plague and a monumental fire – the 'Great Fire of London' – in 1666. This led to large amounts of the city needing to be rebuilt and designed. London also experienced conflict during the English civil war.

London developed significantly during the Industrial Revolution in the nineteenth century and expanded rapidly with increasing levels of migration of people from the surrounding countryside to the city. Towards the end of the Industrial Revolution, London developed an underground train network, the Tube, which is the oldest in the world.

During the twentieth century, London was bombed extensively in the Second World War. After the war, London experienced large waves of migration, which made the city more multicultural and diverse. The city is a global financial centre and continues to grow outwards. In recent years, London has experienced the challenges of terrorist attacks with a series of bomb attacks in 2005. In 2012, London hosted the Olympic Games, bringing further changes and opportunities to the city.

■ **Figure 4.9** Big Ben and the Houses of Parliament, London

ACTIVITY: When disaster strikes

■ ATL

■ Critical-thinking skills – Draw reasonable conclusions and generalizations

1 What is the **origin** and **purpose** of Source A and Source B? How useful do you think these sources would be to someone studying the Great Fire of London?
2 What do Source C and Source D suggest about the different ways that Londoners have dealt with disasters in the past?
3 Reflect – how do you think wars, conflict and disasters could affect different settlements?

SOURCE A

■ **Figure 4.10** A painting of the Great Fire of London

SOURCE B

Extract about the Great Fire of London, recorded by Samuel Pepys in his diary during the time of the fire in 1666

'...all over the Thames, with one's face in the wind you were almost burned with a shower of Firedrops – this is very true – so as houses were burned by these drops and flakes of fire, three or four, nay five or six houses, one from another. When we could endure no more upon the water, we to a little alehouse on the Bankside over against the Three Cranes, and there stayed till it was dark almost and saw the fire grow; and as it grow darker, appeared more and more, and, in Corners and upon steeples and between churches and houses, as far as we could see up the hill of the city, in a most horrid malicious bloody flame, not like the fine flame of an ordinary fire.

'We stayed till, it being darkish, we saw the fire as only one entire arch of fire from this to the other side of the bridge, and in a bow up the hill, for an arch of above a mile long. It made me weep to see it. The churches, houses, and all on fire and flaming at once, and a horrid noise the flames made, and the cracking of houses at their ruin.'

SOURCE C

■ **Figure 4.11** Londoners taking shelter in the Underground during the Blitz, 1940–41

SOURCE D

■ **Figure 4.12** A man wearing a T-shirt with the words 'Still not scared' in the aftermath of the terrorist attacks in London in 2005

CASE STUDY 3 – MEXICO CITY, MEXICO

Founded by the Aztecs and originally known as Tenochtitlan, Mexico City has grown considerably over the centuries to become a prominent city in Latin America.

The Aztec city was taken over by the Spanish in the sixteenth century, who immediately began to influence the design and architecture of the city. After independence from Spain in the early nineteenth century, Mexico City continued to act as the most significant settlement in the country.

During the nineteenth century, the city experienced warfare in the Mexico-American war and was captured for a time.

Over the past hundred years, Mexico City has grown considerably and is now one of the largest cities in the world; it is officially a megacity. The growth of population has brought a variety of challenges to the city including overcrowding and crime. In 1985, an earthquake struck causing damage to large parts of the city.

Every year, people in the city celebrate the 'Day of the Dead' to pay respect and support to family and friends who have died; it is an important cultural tradition in the city and throughout the country of Mexico.

■ **Figure 4.13** Mexico City panorama

Individuals & Societies for the IB MYP 1: *by Concept*

■ **Figure 4.14a** Traditional Aztec dance to celebrate the founding of Mexico City as Tenochtitlan

■ **Figure 4.14b** Figurines used to celebrate the 'Day of the Dead' annual festival in Mexico

■ **Figure 4.14c** A family collects water in a poor neighbourhood of the city

REFLECTION

Based on the three case studies and your own knowledge, write a reflection based on the following conceptual question – '**How do settlements change over time?**' Try to consider the impact of the following factors on settlement: economic, political, environmental, cultural and social.

WHAT MAKES YOU SAY THAT?

Look at the pictures of Mexico City (Figure 4.14a–c). What does each picture reveal about the identity of Mexico City? What makes you say that?

Types of changes

When exploring the key concept of change a useful skill to develop is the identification of different types of changes. Here are some examples:
- SOCIAL – These are changes associated with society and the lives of ordinary people.
- ECONOMIC – These changes are usually financial in nature and are to do with the flow of money as well as trade and exchange.
- POLITICAL – These changes are often to do with governments, who rules a particular place and different policies that are passed.
- ENVIRONMENTAL – This type of change is to do with both human and natural environments and how they can have an impact on different events and processes.
- CULTURAL – This type of change might be to do with people's identities and beliefs or different artistic movements.

What is urban growth?

What is migration?

Migration refers to the movement of people from place to place. Some people are nomadic which means that they are always moving from place to place and tend to live only in temporary settlements, as discussed at the start of the chapter. Other people migrate at different times in their lives. For example, a young person might migrate temporarily to a specific city to attend a university; other people migrate for economic opportunities, which usually involve higher-paid work.

Cities tend to offer a lot more job opportunities than rural areas so in recent years the number of people living in cities has increased dramatically. This is known as rural to urban migration.

Urban growth refers to the development and growth of towns and cities. Today, most people live in cities so the study of urban environments is important in understanding how these types of settlements change and how they provide for people. One reason why towns and cities grow in size is due to the large numbers of people who migrate from rural areas to urban areas. The reasons why people migrate from rural to urban areas can be classified in terms of **push and pull factors**:

Push factors are reasons why people move away from a place. People often leave rural areas in favour of urban areas owing to a lack of jobs, services or social opportunities.

Pull factors are the reasons why people choose to move to a particular place. Urban areas tend to offer a wide range of jobs, services, facilities and social opportunities so they can be more attractive to people as a place to live.

Urban growth has occurred throughout history, but in recent years the number of people living in cities has increased significantly. Approximately half of the global population live in urban areas and this has had an impact on the size of urban areas, including the development of a number of **megacities**.

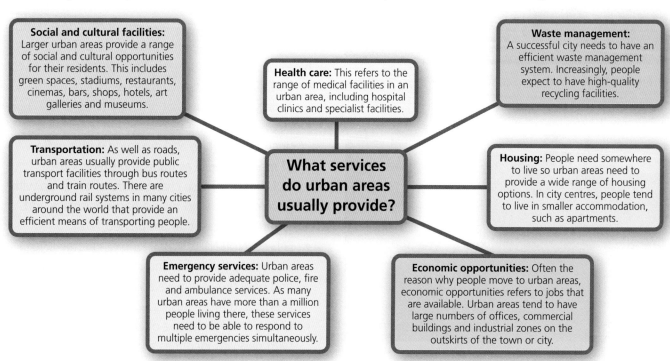

Social and cultural facilities: Larger urban areas provide a range of social and cultural opportunities for their residents. This includes green spaces, stadiums, restaurants, cinemas, bars, shops, hotels, art galleries and museums.

Health care: This refers to the range of medical facilities in an urban area, including hospital clinics and specialist facilities.

Waste management: A successful city needs to have an efficient waste management system. Increasingly, people expect to have high-quality recycling facilities.

Transportation: As well as roads, urban areas usually provide public transport facilities through bus routes and train routes. There are underground rail systems in many cities around the world that provide an efficient means of transporting people.

What services do urban areas usually provide?

Housing: People need somewhere to live so urban areas need to provide a wide range of housing options. In city centres, people tend to live in smaller accommodation, such as apartments.

Emergency services: Urban areas need to provide adequate police, fire and ambulance services. As many urban areas have more than a million people living there, these services need to be able to respond to multiple emergencies simultaneously.

Economic opportunities: Often the reason why people move to urban areas, economic opportunities refers to jobs that are available. Urban areas tend to have large numbers of offices, commercial buildings and industrial zones on the outskirts of the town or city.

■ **Figure 4.15** What services do urban areas usually provide?

ACTIVITY: The growth of cities

■ ATL

Critical-thinking skills – Develop contrary or opposing arguments

1 According to Source A, which city is estimated to increase the most by 2025? What do you think are the reasons for the growth of these cities?
2 Read the following statements. Decide whether they are examples of push factors or pull factors and explain why.
   a On average, the salaries for workers are higher in cities than in rural areas.
   b There are fewer people in rural areas.
   c The city has just opened a new underground train network.
   d Traditional industries in the countryside are in decline.
3 Using the information in the book and your own ideas, complete a SWOT analysis on cities. You can use this template to help you structure your ideas.

STRENGTHS – What do cities do well? What are the strengths of cities? Why do people like living in them?	WEAKNESSES – What are the usual issues or problems associated with cities? Why do some people choose not to live in them?
OPPORTUNITIES – What opportunities could improve the living conditions in cities in the future? What would make more people want to live in cities?	THREATS – What are the possible problems, threats or dangers facing cities in the future? What do cities need to watch out for? Why could cities be undesirable?

■ **Figure 4.16** SWOT analysis

4 Hold a class debate with the question – **'Are cities the future?'** Think about some of the discussion points raised in the information and activity so far. Try to have groups of people arguing in favour of and against the question. You can use your SWOT analysis to help to structure the debate.

◆ Assessment opportunities:

In this activity you have practised skills that are assessed using Criterion D: Thinking critically.

SOURCE A

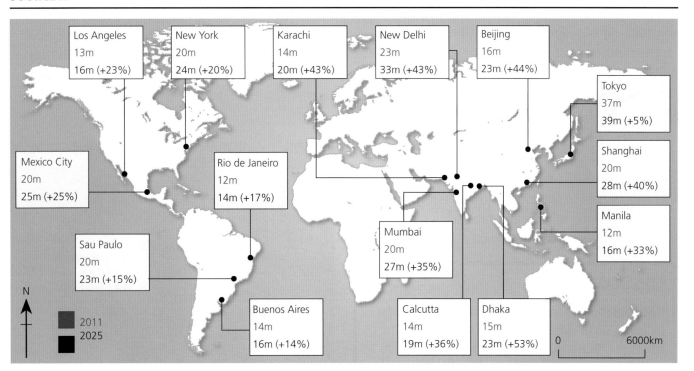

■ **Figure 4.17** The world's fastest growing megacities (population in millions, 2011–25)

Why are some settlements abandoned?

DISCUSS

Search online to find the lyrics of the song 'Ghost Town' by The Specials.

What do you think is meant by the term 'ghost town'?

What do you think is the message of the lyrics of the song?

■ **Figure 4.18** The Specials sang about a 'Ghost Town' in 1980

THE CHALLENGES FACING SETTLEMENTS

Ghost towns are places which used to be busy and thriving settlements but which fell on hard times and no longer function as a sufficient or sustainable settlement. For a variety of reasons these settlements are gradually or suddenly abandoned and people no longer choose to live there. However, there are also settlements that exist with very low population levels; this presents challenges for the settlements as often they are unable to provide the economic opportunities or facilities that would encourage growth.

There are a number of reasons why settlements become abandoned or gradually depopulate: for instance, people might migrate from the town to a nearby city owing to economic factors like gaining employment. This is quite common as cities do tend to provide more of these opportunities. Other settlements may lose a particular industry; for example, many mining towns used to be busy industrial towns but have fallen into disrepair as mines have been closed due to diminished resources or lack of efficiency. Settlements can also be struck by disaster, which makes them inhospitable places. Settlements may be abandoned at times of war, by the impact of natural disasters or other types of crisis. A falling **birth rate** can also lead to settlements struggling to sustain themselves, if the numbers of people living there are too small.

DISCUSS

Depopulation of settlements can also be caused by lower birth rates. We will discuss population issues in Chapter 6. What challenges might face a society if the birth rate becomes very low? Could there be any benefits to the society?

■ **Figure 4.19** Abandoned bumper cars in the city of Pripyat, Ukraine

ACTIVITY: Short film about abandoned settlements

This is a creative task to **explore**, through the use of film, an example of a settlement that has become abandoned. You need to select an example of a settlement and then produce a script to **explain** the reasons why it became abandoned. Research the conditions of the settlement before it became abandoned and why it became abandoned. Finally, present your findings in the form of a documentary or film.

Possible case studies:
- **Pripyat, Ukraine**
- **Bodie, California, USA**
- **Montserrat, Caribbean**
- **Hashima Island, Japan**
- **Pyramiden, Svalbard**
- **Herculaneum, Italy**

CASE STUDY – PRIPYAT, UKRAINE

Pripyat was a small city that provided residence and services to the people who worked in a nuclear power plant at nearby Chernobyl. The city was fully functioning and growing as a settlement until 1986 when an explosion in the nuclear power plant released radioactive material, which had a devastating effect on the people in the surrounding area. As well as the impact leading directly to a number of deaths, the exposure to radiation poisoning affected many people, causing different types of cancer. The radiation fallout was said to have spread to a much wider area than just Pripyat. The city itself needed to be evacuated in order to protect the inhabitants from further contact with the radioactive materials and the city became abandoned.

Today, the radiation levels in the area are still monitored closely and the settlement is still abandoned, though many people visit safe areas of the city for tourism purposes to see first hand this abandoned settlement. The story of Pripyat shows how quickly a settlement can become abandoned when disaster strikes.

CASE STUDY – BODIE, USA

Bodie, named after the gold prospector WS Bodey, developed as a settlement in the mid-nineteenth century due to the discovery of gold in the area. Gold was mined in a number of settlements on the west coast of the USA, triggering a **gold rush** that particularly affected California. The reserves of gold in and around Bodie attracted many people to settle in the town and it developed significantly towards the end of the nineteenth century, providing various services including a bank, saloons and a prison. As a Wild West town it had its fair share of criminal activity.

The town reached its peak in the 1870s and then began a slow decline due to the diminishing reserves of gold. Many prospectors left the town in search of riches elsewhere and Bodie gradually depopulated.

The town today is a significant historic landmark of the gold rush era in the USA and is viewed as a traditional Wild West town. The story of Bodie shows how the availability of resources can lead to both the development and decline of settlements.

■ **Figure 4.20** Abandoned buildings in the town of Bodie, California

How can settlements be more sustainable?

In the planning and designing of new communities, housing projects, and urban renewal, the planners both private and public, need to give explicit consideration to the kind of world that is being created for the children who will be growing up in these settings.

Urie Brofenbrenner, 1973

In 2015, the United Nations launched the '17 Global Goals for Sustainable Development', as mentioned in Chapter 1. One of the targets of these 17 global development goals is to create more 'sustainable cities and communities'. That is, to make settlements more able to be self-reliant and efficient systems for promoting the positive well-being of their citizens.

Sustainability can be promoted in many ways and often involves more use of green technologies. These make the imprint of the city less damaging to the environment and in theory should be more economically efficient. Figure 4.21 shows examples of different ways that cities have implemented sustainable practices into their day-to-day running.

■ **Figure 4.21** Sustainable practices for cities

■ **Figure 4.22** A skate park in Frankfurt in a restored industrial area of the city

FRANKFURT, GERMANY – A SUSTAINABLE CITY?

The city of Frankfurt, in Germany, was recently named as the most sustainable city in the world owing to its practices that look to improve the quality of life for people living there.

The city has created a green belt within the city centre – with substantial cycle tracks, and green spaces for leisure and recreation. Many older industrial areas have been converted into usable spaces. For instance, there are skateboarding parks in the old shipyard area.

There are also a range of energy-saving schemes including more widespread use of renewable energy, more opportunity for cycling to reduce the use of cars, and green buildings that are designed to use less energy. The city has given itself the target to be run 100 per cent by renewable energy sources by 2050. There is also an emphasis on environmental education to ensure the continuation of these practices in future years.

! Take action

! Develop more sustainable practices in your school

! A good place to start with sustainability is in your local area and even closer is your school community. There are a number of things that can be done to make a school more sustainable in terms of its energy use, environmental impact and effect on the well-being of all people who study and work there.

! Think about the following questions to help you to develop your action project:
♦ What does the term 'sustainable' mean to you?

♦ What projects could you carry out to improve the sustainability of the school? What difference do you think they would make?

♦ What are some of the ways that communities can become more sustainable?

SUMMATIVE ASSESSMENT TASK: A settlement of your choice

For this task, you need to write a 500–800 word response to one of the following prompts:

- **Describe** the factors that led to the creation and early development of [your settlement].
- **Explain** how [your settlement] changed over time.
- **Identify** the opportunities and challenges facing [your settlement] today.
- **Explore** the different ways that [your settlement] can be described as sustainable.

You need to choose a question and a settlement to work on. For instance, if you decided to look at Paris, France, and you chose the last question, your research question would be: **Explore** the different ways that Paris can be described as sustainable. Alternatively, if you decided to focus on Sydney, Australia, and the first question, your research question would be: **Describe** the factors that led to the creation and early development of Sydney.

For this task you are being assessed against Criterion B: Investigating so you will need to create an action plan. In this you need to include your chosen research question and an explanation of why you chose it. The justification of why you chose the question must show a reflection of why you felt it was significant or interesting. Your action plan should also include your research and organization in preparation for writing this task.

Each of the questions has a highlighted command term. The definitions below will help you gain an idea of how to structure your response depending on which command term you have.

The command terms for this task are highlighted below.

Describe – Give a detailed account or picture of a situation, event, pattern or process.

Explain – Give a detailed account including reasons or causes.

Identify – Provide an answer from a number of possibilities. Recognize and state briefly a distinguishing fact or feature.

Explore – Undertake a systematic process of discovery.

Definitions from IB MYP Individuals and societies guide, *2014*

This task is also assessed against Criterion C: Communicating. Therefore, you should focus on writing in a clear and coherent manner with good organization. You should also include a bibliography of the sources that you have used in the process of researching your question.

◆ Assessment opportunities:

This activity can be assessed using Criterion B: Investigating (strands i, ii and iii) and Criterion C: Communicating (strands i, ii and ii).

Reflection

As we have seen in this chapter, settlements develop and change due to a variety of factors; some settlements are only temporary while others go from strength to strength. In recent years, more and more people are choosing to live in cities, bringing both opportunities and challenges. Sustainability represents a good option for different societies to improve the quality of life for the people living there and for future generations to come.

Use this table to reflect on your own learning in this chapter		
Questions we asked	Answers we found	Any further questions now?
Factual What are the different types of settlement? What makes a good location for a settlement? What is meant by urbanization? Why are some settlements abandoned?		
Conceptual How do settlements change over time? How can settlements be more sustainable?		
Debatable Are cities the future?		

Approaches to learning you used in this chapter	Description – what new skills did you learn?	How well did you master the skills?			
		Novice	Learner	Practitioner	Expert
Communication skills					
Creative-thinking skills					
Critical-thinking skills					
Information literacy skills					

Learner profile attribute(s)	Reflect on the importance of being a communicator for your learning in this chapter.
Communicator	

5 What do people believe in?

Belief systems provide **guidance** to people in different ways and can **shape personal identity and culture**.

■ **Figure 5.1** (*l–r*) Lalibela Church in Ethiopia; Zen Garden in Kyoto, Japan; a Native American totem pole in Stanley Park, Vancouver, Canada; a Hindu woman praying in the river Ganges, India

CONSIDER THESE QUESTIONS:

Factual: What are the beliefs of the major world religions? What is indigenous belief? What examples are there of non-religious belief?

Conceptual: How does belief change over time? How can identity be shaped by personal belief?

Debatable: To what extent does belief cloud or clarify our judgement? Is it possible to believe in nothing?

Now **share and compare** your thoughts and ideas with your partner, or with the whole class.

○ IN THIS CHAPTER WE WILL …

■ **Find out:**
  ■ about the beliefs of the major world religions
  ■ about indigenous belief with specific examples
  ■ how belief can affect people's identity and actions.
■ **Explore:**
  ■ religious beliefs of Buddhism, Islam, Hinduism, Judaism and Christianity
  ■ indigenous beliefs including animism
  ■ ways of thinking that are concerned with spiritual powers.
■ **Take action** by finding ways to promote tolerance and understanding of people who may have beliefs different from our own.

SEE–THINK–WONDER

Look at the pictures in Figure 5.1. What do you see? What do you think the connection is between each picture and belief? What does it make you wonder?

INTRODUCING BELIEF

Human societies have long grappled with the big questions about the world around them. Why are we here? How was the universe created? How should we live our lives? These questions have, over time, shaped numerous belief systems that look to find answers to these questions and provide guidance to people in different ways. We can define belief as something that people strongly think to be true. It can shape personal identity as it can often have an impact on lifestyle and the choices made in daily life.

THINK–PAIR–SHARE

What do you believe in? Make your own list and then share your ideas with a partner.

What are the beliefs of the major world religions?

Religious belief is common around the world, with more than 80 per cent of the world's population following a wide variety of different religions. Religion often impacts on the way that people live their lives as the different religions provide guidance and teaching for ways to live. Examples of this include how someone might dress, the food that is eaten, and the different rituals and routines associated with prayer.

DISCUSS

Go back to the partner you worked with earlier. Make another list, this time of different ways that religious belief could affect someone's lifestyle and routines. Try to think of specific examples from your own knowledge.

ⓘ Different theisms

Religion usually involves believing in something that you can't actually prove; sometimes this involves one or multiple gods depending on the specific religion. A **theism** relates to different beliefs about the existence of god.

- Polytheism – the belief in or worship of more than one god
- Monotheism – the belief in or worship of one God
- Atheism – the belief that there is no god
- Pantheism – the belief that there is a supreme god who forms a part of everything.

ACTIVITY: World religions

■ ATL

- Critical-thinking skills – Draw reasonable conclusions and generalizations

Interpret Table 5.1 and the map (Figure 5.2) and answer the following questions.

1 **Which religion has the largest number of followers worldwide?**
2 **What are some of the major similarities and differences between the different religions?**
3 **Some religions can be found in many different places over the world map. Why do you think this has happened? What factors would have contributed to the spread of religion?**
4 **What do you think is meant on the map by 'traditional and tribal religions'?**
5 **From the map, try to identify any divisions within the major religious groups.**
6 **Write a list of questions that you would like to know the answers to after looking at the map and table to develop your inquiry further.**

◆ Assessment opportunities:

In this activity you have practised skills that are assessed using Criterion A: Knowing and understanding.

EXTENSION

In this chapter we will profile some of the major world religions but what about some of the other religions? Here are some examples that you could find out about: Shinto, Sikhism, Jainism, Daoism.

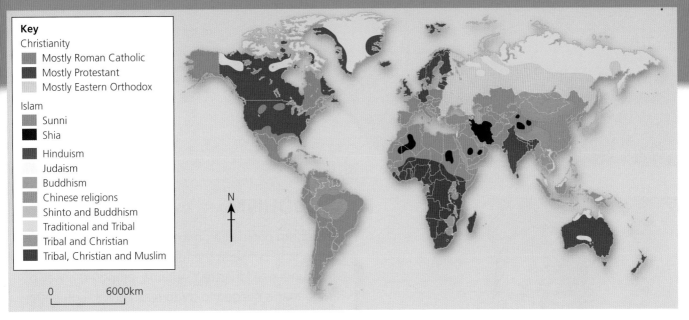

■ **Figure 5.2** Map of the distribution of world religions

■ **Table 5.1** Summary information about some of the major world religions

Religion	Origins	Followers (approximate)	Beliefs	Rituals and practices
Buddhism	Founded in the late sixth century BCE by Siddhartha Gautama (the Buddha).	488 million	The Four Noble Truths and following the Eightfold Noble Path to achieve 'nirvana' or enlightenment.	Meditation, generosity and compassion to others.
Christianity	Founded around 30CE by Jesus Christ in modern day Israel.	2 billion	One God, Jesus Christ as the son of God. Jesus was sacrificed to save humans from the sins they commit.	Prayer, worship in church. Celebrate Easter and Christmas. Sunday as day of rest (Sabbath).
Hinduism	Developed in the Indian subcontinent – considered to be one of the earliest religions in the world. Hinduism is a collection of belief systems that gathered together over the years.	900 million	Samsara – cycle of birth, life and death. Trimurti – Brahma the creator, Vishnu the preserver and Shiva the destroyer.	Yoga, meditation, worship, pilgrimage. Various dietary laws, e.g. many Hindus are vegetarian and nearly all will not eat beef.
Islam	Founded on the Arabian peninsular in the seventh century CE by the Prophet Muhammad.	1.3 billion	One God (Allah), Muhammad is the messenger of God. Five Pillars of Islam.	Five Pillars of Islam including prayer five times daily; worship in a mosque. Food and drink should be halal and pork and alcohol are not consumed.
Judaism	The Hebrew religion began with a covenant between God and Abraham, who was an early founder of the religion.	14 million	One God (Yahweh). Live ethically and with principles. Following the different covenants that are explained in the Torah, the religious book of Judaism.	Worship in synagogue. Day of rest from Friday evening to Saturday evening (Shabbat). Eat kosher food.

BUDDHISM

Buddhism originated on the Indian subcontinent some time between the fourth and sixth century BCE. Its founder, Siddhartha Gautama, proposed a way of living that is needed to try to reach enlightenment or **nirvana**. By achieving this one can live a life that avoids suffering. Gautama is referred to as 'the Buddha' and Buddhism has grown to be the fourth largest religion in the world.

Buddhism provides suggestions about how to live a more meaningful life. Some of the suggestions include the importance of meditation and mindfulness. Buddhism advocates stricter self-control and the avoidance of impulsiveness. The key teaching is to try to find the 'Middle Way' in life, to find balance. This can be achieved by neither allowing oneself to be tempted by greed nor by being overly strict and denying oneself the things needed in life.

■ **Figure 5.3** A Buddhist monk meditating

SEE–THINK–WONDER

Study the picture in Figure 5.3. What do you see? What do you think about that? What does it make you wonder?

DISCUSS

Look at the following behaviours:
- **Anger**
- **Fasting often, very rarely eating food**
- **Listening carefully to others**
- **Reflecting on lifestyle**
- **Working hard at a job to gain more and more money**
- **Compassion for others**
- **Swearing.**

Identify examples of Buddhist thought and behaviour from the list and **explain** why they are examples.

The principles of Buddhism place emphasis on the elimination of suffering through following the Four Noble Truths and living life through the Noble Eightfold Path (the Middle Way).

Most of the followers of Buddhism live in Asia, especially South East and East Asia. Buddhism has also developed in Western countries.

DISCUSS

Black Friday

Black Friday is the Friday following Thanksgiving (the fourth Thursday of November), and has become known as the beginning of the Christmas shopping season. It originally started in the USA but has now spread to other parts of the world. Most of the major shops open early (and recently, overnight) offering promotional sales.

Use these search terms to view pictures and videos of the mayhem: Black Friday queues.

In pairs, **discuss** why you think people are queuing. What do you think Buddhists might say about this?

ⓘ The Four Noble Truths

1 **DUKKHA** – There is suffering and dissatisfaction in the world.
   An important feature of Dukkha is the realization that suffering is not always physical suffering. Most often, suffering refers to people's feelings that they are dissatisfied with their lives, such as they might want to earn more money, or they may be jealous of their friends. This suffering, according to Buddhism, is a big problem for trying to find the Middle Way.

2 **SAMUDAYA** – Suffering is caused by our desires and attachments.
   Gautama's teaching emphasized that the root cause of virtually all suffering can be linked to wanting and desire. Consequently, greedy thoughts about new material possessions would be the cause of some examples of suffering.

3 **NIRODHA** – Suffering can be eliminated.
   This can be explained through Gautama's realization that by removing Samudaya from one's life, suffering can be eliminated. This refers to the ability to detach ourselves from our desires, wants and cravings. Buddhists emphasize the importance of moderation in daily life.

4 **MAGGA** – Suffering is eliminated by following the Noble Eightfold Path.
   The final truth, Magga, offers a guide to life for Buddhists. This guide is the Noble Eightfold Path or Middle Way. This guides Buddhists in how to live through three key areas:
   • Wisdom (stages 1, 2, 3)
   • Morality (stages 4, 5, 6)
   • Concentration (stages 7, 8).

The Noble Eightfold Path

SEE–THINK–WONDER

Look at Figure 5.4 and think about what the Noble Eightfold Path demonstrates. In groups, brainstorm ways one might live in order to honour the Eightfold Path. Do you think this would be easy or difficult? Why do you think this?

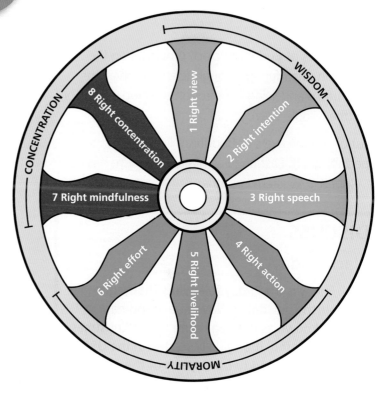

■ **Figure 5.4** The Noble Eightfold Path

Samsara

One of the important beliefs of Buddhism is that of interconnectedness – a belief that there are causes and consequences for all things that happen in life. The awareness of cause and consequence allows Buddhists to reflect on where suffering may come from so that they can make changes to avoid it. Buddhism, like Hinduism, also puts forward the belief in the concept of **samsara**, the endless cycle of birth, life and death. Buddhists believe that the cycle can be broken by trying to achieve nirvana (enlightenment), by following the Noble Eightfold Path.

An important tool for Buddhist understanding of samsara is called the Wheel of Life. The Wheel of Life shows the cycle of birth, life and death that every living thing is trapped in. In the centre of the wheel are three animals: a cockerel representing greed, a snake representing hate and a pig representing ignorance. The wheel is held by a monstrous figure representing death. Buddhists believe that it is possible to escape this cycle by following the Noble Eightfold Path.

DISCUSS

Look at the details on the Wheel of Life (Figure 5.5). What do you think is happening at the different sections of the wheel?

■ **Figure 5.5** The Wheel of Life

Buddhism developed into two main strands:

- Theravada, meaning 'Teaching of the Elders', is largely practised in Laos, Myanmar, Cambodia and Sri Lanka.
- Mahayana, meaning 'The Great Vehicle', is practised across East Asia including China, Japan and Korea.

A particularly well-known strand of Buddhism is Zen Buddhism, which is largely practised in East Asia, especially in Korea and Japan. This strand particularly focuses on the importance of knowing yourself and places emphasis on meditation and reflection.

Three key profiles in Buddhism

Siddhartha Gautama 'the Buddha'

Born into royalty in northern India, close to Nepal, Siddhartha Gautama was protected by his father who did not want him to see the problems of the world and showered him with gifts and comforts throughout his life. When Gautama finally left the comforts of his palace, he observed suffering in the form of 'old age', 'sickness' and 'death'. Shocked by this revelation he sought inspiration from holy men on how to live life with the knowledge that suffering is inevitable.

Gautama came to the realization that to be able to live in peace, a sense of compassion and selflessness was needed in order to reach nirvana. He taught the importance of living a balanced life with the Four Noble Truths and the Noble Eightfold Path as key teachings.

■ **Figure 5.6** Siddhartha Gautama 'the Buddha'

Ashoka the Great

Ashoka was an Indian emperor who held great power over the Indian subcontinent in the third century BCE. He controlled vast swathes of land and won many wars. He converted to Buddhism which at the time had only a small following. Ashoka is credited with being the figure who spread the influence of Buddhism across large areas of East and South East Asia.

■ **Figure 5.7** Ashoka the Great

The Dalai Lama

The Dalai Lama is the contemporary spiritual leader of Buddhism, specifically Tibetan Buddhism. The current Dalai Lama is Tenzin Gyatso who was born in 1935 but was exiled from Tibet in 1950 after the People's Republic of China took control of the region. He is a revered figure to Buddhists around the world.

■ **Figure 5.8** The Dalai Lama

ACTIVITY: Postcard about Buddhism

■ **ATL**

Communication skills – Use appropriate forms of writing for different purposes and audiences

Write a postcard to a student in a younger year group than you are in. Choose an appropriate picture to go on one side of the postcard. On the other side, write an explanation in your own words of what Buddhism is. Think about the origins and the key teachings. Aim to write between 50 and 100 words only.

◆ **Assessment opportunities:**

In this activity you have practised skills that are assessed using Criterion C: Communicating.

DISCUSS

Look at the tweets from the current Dalai Lama (Figure 5.9).

What additional ideas can you gain about Buddhism from the different tweets from the current Dalai Lama?

Look at his Twitter account to find more examples.

Tweets   Tweets & replies   Photos & videos

Dalai Lama @DalaiLama
Deep down we must have a real affection for each other, a clear recognition of our shared status as human beings.
↩   ♻ 857   ♥ 1.4K   •••

Dalai Lama @DalaiLama
Friends are made on the basis of trust and trust only grows if you are kind to people.
↩   ♻ 1205   ♥ 3.2K   •••

Dalai Lama @DalaiLama
When our mind is calm, we're better able to find peace of mind and live a joyful life.
↩   ♻ 984   ♥ 2.7K   •••

Dalai Lama @DalaiLama
We need to strike a balance between material and spiritual progress, a balance achieved on the basis of love and compassion.
↩   ♻ 1562   ♥ 1.9K   •••

■ **Figure 5.9** Selected Tweets from the Dalai Lama

REFLECTION

How do you think following Buddhism would affect an individual's identity and perspective?

ISLAM

Islam is a major world religion with more than a billion followers worldwide. The followers of Islam are called Muslims. The religion of Islam is divided into two major branches, that of Sunni and Shi'a traditions.

Islam as a religion originated on the Arabian peninsula and has spread to many regions of the world. Islam is a monotheistic religion, with belief in one God (the Arabic word for God is Allah), and the teachings of the religion can be found in the holy book, the Qur'an.

There is debate over the exact origins of the Islamic faith, but the general consensus is that the religion became established through the teachings and life of the Prophet Muhammad in the seventh century CE. According to the Islamic faith, Muhammad received messages from God (Allah) through the Angel Jibrail (Arabic for Gabriel) and these messages were later written down as the Qur'an.

Muhammad was said to have been visited several times by the Angel Jibrail and Muslims view Muhammad as the final messenger of God.

■ **Figure 5.10** Depiction of the Angel Jibrail (Gabriel) from 'The Wonders of Creation and the Oddities of Existence', a manuscript created in the late fourteenth century

The Qur'an

The Qur'an was created to contain the messages or revelations that the Prophet Muhammad received during his lifetime. The book covers a wide range of issues including advice on how to live a good life. The book is not arranged in chronological order or written as a narrative.

The chapters of the Qur'an make reference to different themes. Each chapter is known as a surah, of which there are more than a hundred, and each has a different name, including 'The Elephant', 'The Moon' and 'The Thunder'.

The Qur'an is a highly revered book for Muslims and there are a number of rituals attached to using the book. For example, it must always be kept on clean surfaces as a mark of respect, it is often carried in a bag to keep it clean and when placed on a bookshelf it must be on the highest shelf with no other book above it.

■ **Figure 5.11** The Qur'an

The Five Pillars of Islam

A very important aspect of Islam, and the five main ways in which Muslims worship, is called the Five Pillars of Islam (see Figure 5.12 for more details).

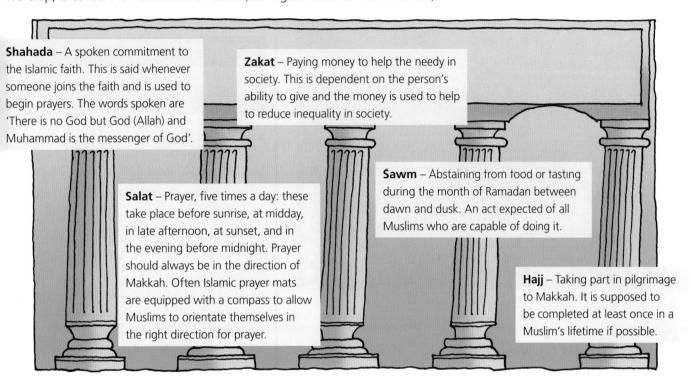

Shahada – A spoken commitment to the Islamic faith. This is said whenever someone joins the faith and is used to begin prayers. The words spoken are 'There is no God but God (Allah) and Muhammad is the messenger of God'.

Zakat – Paying money to help the needy in society. This is dependent on the person's ability to give and the money is used to help to reduce inequality in society.

Salat – Prayer, five times a day: these take place before sunrise, at midday, in late afternoon, at sunset, and in the evening before midnight. Prayer should always be in the direction of Makkah. Often Islamic prayer mats are equipped with a compass to allow Muslims to orientate themselves in the right direction for prayer.

Sawm – Abstaining from food or fasting during the month of Ramadan between dawn and dusk. An act expected of all Muslims who are capable of doing it.

Hajj – Taking part in pilgrimage to Makkah. It is supposed to be completed at least once in a Muslim's lifetime if possible.

■ **Figure 5.12** The Five Pillars of Islam

DISCUSS

Look at Figure 5.13. Which of the five pillars are represented in the painting?

■ **Figure 5.13** 'The Muezzin in his Minaret calling the Faithful to Prayer', 1926

■ **Figure 5.14** Hajj to Makkah

ℹ️
Pilgrimage to Makkah

The pilgrimage (called Hajj) to Makkah in Saudi Arabia is an important experience for Muslims around the world. The Hajj takes place each year during the month of Dhu all-Hijjah and follows a route that takes pilgrims to a variety of sacred locations in and around the city of Makkah.

Figure 5.14 shows the Kaaba, a sacred site of the Islamic religion. The Kaaba is the black cube in the middle of the Grand Mosque. When Muslims arrive at the Grand Mosque they walk around it seven times in an anti-clockwise direction. At the beginning of each circuit they also try to get as close as possible to the Black Stone that is placed in one corner of the Kaaba.

Other parts of the Hajj include drinking water from the well at Zamzam, spending the night in an open plains area called Muzdalifa and performing a ritual called the 'stoning of the Devil' where Muslims throw pebbles at three pillars in the town of Mina near Makkah.

ACTIVITY: Pilgrimage guide

■ ATL

Transfer skills – Inquire in different contexts to gain a different perspective

- **What do you understand by the term 'pilgrimage'?**
- **How do you think taking part in an experience like the Hajj might affect someone?**

Choose an example of a well-known pilgrimage route in the world, for instance:
- **Lumbini in Nepal for Buddhists**
- **Cathedral of Santiago de Compostela in Spain for Christians**
- **Golden Temple in Amritsar in India for Sikhs**
- **Makkah in Saudi Arabia for Muslims.**

Create a guide for people who are about to take part in your chosen pilgrimage. Include useful information about the religious significance of some of the locations, reasons why people take part in these pilgrimages, the traditions and the route. **Explain** how participation in pilgrimage might affect the people involved.

◆ Assessment opportunities:

In this activity you have practised skills that are assessed using Criterion A: Knowing and understanding (strands i and ii) and Criterion C: Communicating (strands i, ii and iii).

The Golden Age of Islam

After the death of the Prophet Muhammad in 632CE, the Islamic religion continued to expand rapidly and a series of caliphates (the name given to an Islamic government that is run by a leader who is said to be a successor of Muhammad) took control over areas across the Middle East, North Africa, Southern Europe and Central Asia.

The time period of the seventh and eighth centuries CE became known as the 'Golden Age of Islam' as scholarship flourished with particular developments in the arts, sciences, mathematics and literature.

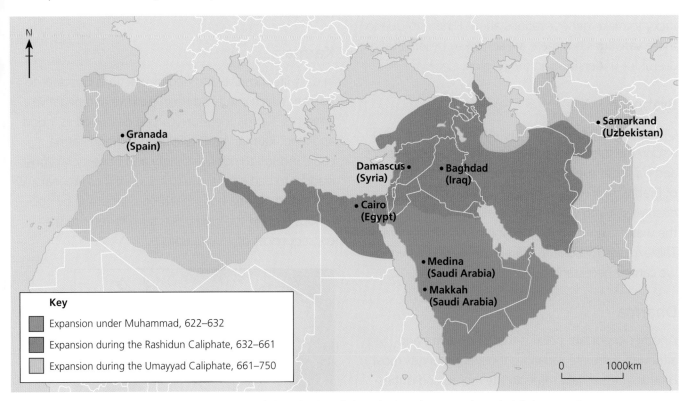

■ **Figure 5.15** Map showing the expansion of the Islamic religion during the seventh and eighth centuries CE

Sharia Law

During this Golden Age, cities developed considerably. These cities became great centres for architecture, trade and cultural developments. In these cities, legal systems evolved that were based on Islamic teachings; this law became known as Sharia Law. Although there are variations within its application owing to differing Islamic traditions, it generally refers to moral laws for everyday life. Sharia Law is still in use today in a number of countries in the world; these include Saudi Arabia, United Arab Emirates and Brunei.

DISCUSS

Why might religious beliefs influence legal systems? What opportunities and challenges might this bring about?

DISCUSS

What do you think is the message of the cartoon in Figure 5.16?

Could you make a connection between this picture and the concept of karma?

How might belief in karma affect an individual's actions in life?

HINDUISM

Hinduism is an ancient religion originating on the Indian subcontinent. It has more than 900 million followers in the world today. The word Hinduism actually refers to and encompasses multiple religions that have evolved in the region over time. It is quite tricky to make generalizations about Hinduism due to these variations but there are some key beliefs that are useful for understanding the religion.

Brahman

One of the key beliefs of Hinduism is the existence of a supreme ruler God, Brahman, who effectively forms and is part of everything. To understand the nature of Brahman, an old Indian legend tells of how if you dissolve salt into water you will always taste the salt in the water even though you cannot see it or separate it. This explains the idea that Brahman is everywhere but we cannot necessarily see him.

Dharma

Another important belief is that of **dharma** and although there are variations it generally unites most Hindus. It essentially refers to the morals and duties of Hindus to live a good life, with an emphasis on harmony. It guides Hindus to make good decisions in their daily life and live life with an emphasis on morals and duty to others.

Samsara

Samsara is a belief shared with Buddhists and Sikhs, and refers to the cycle of birth, life and death. The actions and deeds done in one's life have an effect on the future destiny of the next life. This is the idea of

reincarnation – the cycle of life and death and the determination of what future lives will be like based on your actions. A further important belief related to this is that of **moksha** which is the path to escaping samsara by following the teachings of Hinduism and living life according to the **Vedas** (the sacred writings of Hinduism).

Karma

In daily life, positive and negative actions can refer to **karma**, which can build up in positive and negative amounts. Karma therefore can be described as 'good' and 'bad' karma. Actions leading to good karma could include things like charity and honesty; actions leading to bad karma could include things like jealousy and greed. Karma has gained popular usage by non-Hindus around the world as a term to refer to the consequences of your actions.

■ **Figure 5.16** A political cartoon called 'It Shoots Further Than He Dreams' by John F. Knott, 1918

Worship

Worship in Hinduism varies greatly but it is an important part of the religion. Hindus often worship different deities (gods) – some examples of Hindu gods are profiled in Figure 5.16 on pages 114–116.

ACTIVITY: Profile of a Hindu deity

■ ATL

Information literacy skills Construct a bibliography according to recognized conventions

Put together a profile of one Hindu deity of your choice. You could choose one of the examples provided in this chapter or find out about another. Examples of other Hindu deities include: Lakshmi, Saraswati or Durga.

Try to include information on the god's appearance and role in the religion, and any stories about the god. You could also include a picture.

Keep a record of where you find the information and put these references into a bibliography to hand in with your profile.

◆ Assessment opportunities:

In this activity you have practised skills that are assessed using Criterion C: Communicating (strands i, ii and iii).

Creating a bibliography

Bibliographies are used to show the reader where you accessed information when you were researching or reading about a topic. It is good practice to include a bibliography with your work. At times during the course, your teacher will assess your use of bibliographies through Criterion C: Communicating. Remember to use one format for your bibliography (for example, Harvard or APA). Check that the bibliography is in alphabetical order. When using websites, try to find the name of the person who wrote the article.

Hint

- Images should be referenced from their original source, not Google.
- Use sites such as **www.bibme.org** or **www.easybib.com** to help you out.

EXTENSION

Have a go at adding references to your next piece of work.

Hindu gods

The third member of the Trimurti is **Shiva**, who is known as the destroyer god. However although often seen in a destructive capacity, Shiva's destructive role is said to allow for new creations to take place afterwards.

Brahma is not to be confused with 'Brahman', the supreme God.

Brahma is a god in Hinduism. He is part of the Trimurti along with Vishnu and Shiva, which is a trinity of gods who have responsibility for creation, maintenance and destruction of the universe.

Brahma is the creator god and is traditionally seen with four heads and four arms. He is seen carrying prayer beads and a book, and he often rides on the back of a swan.

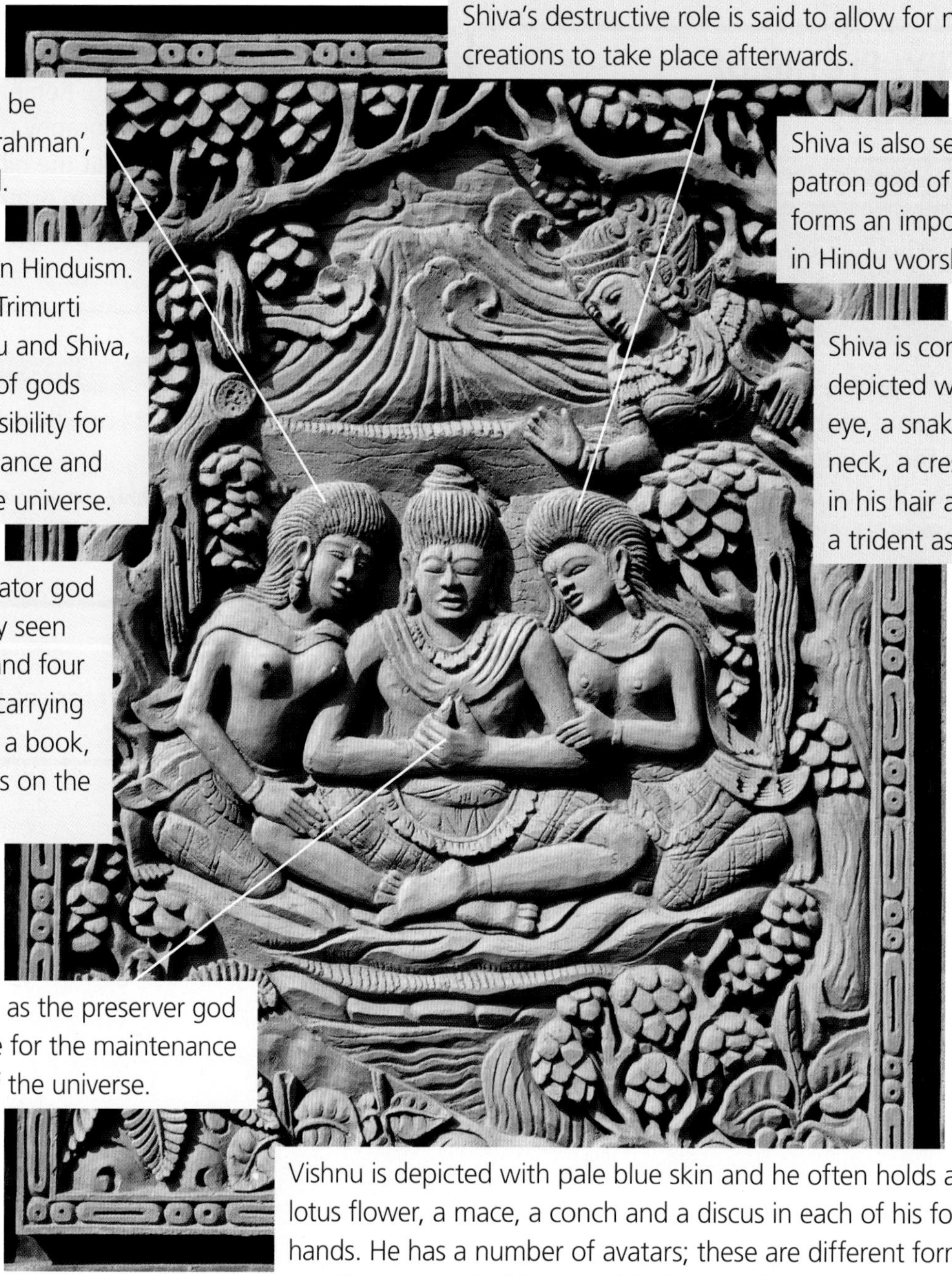

Shiva is also seen as the patron god of yoga, which forms an important ritual in Hindu worship.

Shiva is commonly depicted with a third eye, a snake around his neck, a crescent moon in his hair and carrying a trident as a weapon.

Vishnu is known as the preserver god and is responsible for the maintenance and protection of the universe.

Vishnu is depicted with pale blue skin and he often holds a lotus flower, a mace, a conch and a discus in each of his four hands. He has a number of avatars; these are different forms or manifestations of Vishnu, and include Krishna and Rama.

■ **Figure 5.17a** Brahma, Vishnu and Shiva

Hanuman, the monkey king, is an easily recognizable and popular god in Hinduism. He featured in the Indian poem *Ramayana*, an important piece of literature in India, which tells many stories and features examples of Hanuman's adventures and bravery.

■ **Figure 5.17b** Hanuman

Lord Krishna is a sweet and playful Hindu god who is depicted with pale blue skin and is an avatar of Vishnu, so he is also technically part of the Trimurti.

■ **Figure 5.17c** Krishna

Krishna is widely regarded across many branches of Hinduism and he is a very popular god. He features prominently in the 'Bhagavad Gita' (Hindu text) and is often depicted as a young boy playing the flute.

Rama is well liked as he shows mental strength and commitment by being tested to the extreme in many different situations, which he always manages to overcome. He is said to have a strong commitment to dharma.

Rama also features in the *Ramayana* along with Hanuman, and he is the hero of the story. Like Krishna, he is also an avatar of Vishnu.

■ **Figure 5.17d** Rama

Ganesha is often seen riding on the back of a mouse.

■ **Figure 5.17e** Ganesha

Ganesha is probably the best-known Hindu god around the world because of his distinct appearance – he has an elephant's head.

According to popular folklore, Ganesha is the son of the goddess Parvati (wife of Shiva) who moulded him out of sandalwood paste one day. Soon after he was born, she instructed the boy to stand guard while she took a bath. When Shiva returned to see Parvati, the young Ganesha would not let him in, leading to a fight and Ganesha having his head disconnected from his body. On learning that Ganesha was his son from Parvati, Shiva ordered his followers to return with the head of the first living thing they came across. The result was an elephant's head.

Works of literature

Within Hinduism there are a number of works of literature that help to guide the religion. These include the *Ramayana* and *Mahabharata* and the 'Bhagavad Gita'. The 'Bhagavad Gita' (part of the *Mahabharata*) is very popular and provides Hindus with guidance on many things.

Mohandas Karamchand Gandhi (widely known as Mahatma Gandhi), the Indian independence leader, once commented that:

When doubts haunt me and disappointments stare me in the face and I see not one ray of hope on the horizon, I turn to the 'Bhagavad Gita' and find a verse to comfort me; I immediately begin to smile in the midst of overwhelming sorrow.

■ **Figure 5.18** Mahatma Gandhi

THINK–PAIR–SHARE

Think about these questions. Then **discuss** your answers in pairs. Share your ideas and discussion in groups or with the whole class.

1 What does the quotation from Mahatma Gandhi suggest about the importance of the 'Bhagavad Gita' to Hindus?
2 Why are books important for different religions?

CHRISTIANITY

Christianity is the world's largest religion with more than 2 billion followers. It has multiple branches or **denominations**. These include Roman Catholic, Protestant, Eastern Orthodox and Methodist denominations.

Most branches of Christianity agree on a few key aspects of the religion. The key belief is that of the existence of a single God who sent his son Jesus Christ to save humanity from suffering.

The life of Jesus Christ is recorded in the New Testament, the second section of the Bible, which also explores his teachings and the early development of the Christian religion. The first section of the Bible is the Old Testament, which is shared with Judaism, also known as the Hebrew Bible.

Christians believe in a monotheistic God who wants to help people in the world by forgiving them of the sins that they commit in life. The belief is that sin is something which people do and that by asking for forgiveness and demonstrating belief in Jesus Christ, people can achieve salvation.

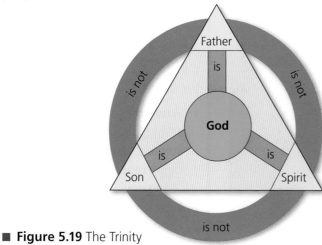

■ **Figure 5.19** The Trinity

Life of Jesus Christ

According to the Christian faith, Jesus was born in the town of Bethlehem in 6BCE. The story of Jesus's birth is told in the Nativity and celebrated by Christians at Christmas on 25 December.

After being baptized by John the Baptist in his early thirties, Jesus began his teachings and performing miracles. During this time, Jesus had a number of **disciples** who were his followers and 12 **apostles** who became important to the establishment of the Christian religion.

According to the New Testament, Jesus's teachings and miracles increasingly threatened the authority of the Roman Empire and he was arrested, beaten and later crucified on a cross. Three days after he died, Jesus is said to have risen from the dead, where he appeared to his disciples for the final time to encourage the teachings and spread of Christianity.

God therefore appears in three different forms, according to Christians, as the **Trinity**: God the father, God the son and God the Holy Spirit.

Christianity is split into several different denominations or branches. Although all denominations are part of the Christian faith, they hold different beliefs and interpretations of aspects of the religion.

The Great Schism

After Christianity became the official religion of the Roman Empire in 380CE, the religious tradition can be associated with that of the Roman Catholic branch. This was later broken into two by an event known as 'The Great Schism' or 'East–West Schism', which essentially divided the Christian faith into the Eastern Orthodox and Roman Catholic denominations.

This had geographic implications as the Eastern Orthodox traditions dominated areas including Russia and Eastern Europe while Roman Catholicism dominated Western Europe and, later, Latin America due to the expansion of Spain and Portugal during the fifteenth and sixteenth centuries.

ACTIVITY: Miracles of Jesus Christ

■ ATL

Communicating skills – Make references and draw conclusions

Read the following extracts from the New Testament.

1 One day as Jesus was standing by the Lake of Gennesaret, with the people crowding around him and listening to the word of God, 2 he saw at the water's edge two boats, left there by the fishermen, who were washing their nets. 3 He got into one of the boats, the one belonging to Simon, and asked him to put out a little from shore. Then he sat down and taught the people from the boat. 4 When he had finished speaking, he said to Simon, "Put out into deep water, and let down the nets for a catch." 5 Simon answered, "Master, we've worked hard all night and haven't caught anything. But because you say so, I will let down the nets." 6 When they had done so, they caught such a large number of fish that their nets began to break. 7 So they signalled their partners in the other boat to come and help them, and they came and filled both boats so full that they began to sink.

LUKE 5: 1–7

15 As evening approached, the disciples came to him and said, "This is a remote place, and it's already getting late. Send the crowds away, so they can go to the villages and buy themselves some food." 16 Jesus replied, "They do not need to go away. You give them something to eat." 17 "We have here only five loaves of bread and two fish," they answered. 18 "Bring them here to me," he said. 19 And he directed the people to sit down on the grass. Taking the five loaves and the two fish and looking up to heaven, he gave thanks and broke the loaves. Then he gave them to the disciples, and the disciples gave them to the people. 20 They all ate and were satisfied, and the disciples picked up twelve basketfuls of broken pieces that were left over. 21 The number of those who ate was about five thousand men, besides women and children.

MATTHEW 14: 15–21

For each story, complete the following tasks:
1 **Summarize** what happened.
2 **Explain** why Christians would describe these events as miracles.

There was further division of Christianity during a historical time period known as the **Reformation**. The Reformation was largely driven by the work of Martin Luther and John Calvin who respectively founded the Lutheran and Calvinist branches of the Protestant faith. In England, King Henry VIII officially broke with the Roman Catholic Church to establish the Church of England, and ordered the Dissolution of the Monasteries.

In recent years, further denominations have been founded including the Jehovah's Witnesses and Mormon churches.

EXTENSION

Research the Protestant Reformation to **explore** the changes affecting Christianity.

DISCUSS

All of the religions we have examined have differing interpretations and subsequently variations in belief. Why do you think this has happened? In pairs, **discuss** the possible reasons why different religions have divisions within them.

JUDAISM

Judaism is approximately 3,500 years old and began with a **covenant** (an agreement) between Abraham and God. Abraham is a very significant figure in the development of religion as he is seen as the first individual to move from the belief of polytheism to monotheism. This was important to the development of Judaism as the first monotheistic religion. Abraham is also an important figure in the development of Christianity and Islam.

This original covenant and subsequent covenants between God and Abraham's descendants form the basis for the Jewish faith. The original covenant was an agreement that if Abraham followed God and his wishes, God would always look after Abraham and his descendants and they would be God's chosen people.

God told Abraham to travel to the land of Canaan (an area in the modern-day Middle East) and this land became the homeland of the Jewish people. This area was part of the 'fertile crescent', which stretched from Egypt through to western Iran and saw the rise of many early civilizations (see Chapter 3).

! **Take action**

! Create a celebration week at your school which showcases the different beliefs and perspectives that exist within your school community. Encourage others to share their personal experiences so as to gain a better understanding of each other.

DISCUSS

The fertile crescent is sometimes referred to as 'the cradle of civilization'. Refer back to the chapter on ancient civilizations (Chapter 3). Why do you think this area led to the development of early civilizations and belief systems?

ACTIVITY: Role-playing the Ten Commandments

■ **ATL**

Communication skills – Interpret and use effectively modes of non-verbal communication

Create a short role play to **demonstrate** one of the Ten Commandments. See if the others in class can guess which commandment you are representing.

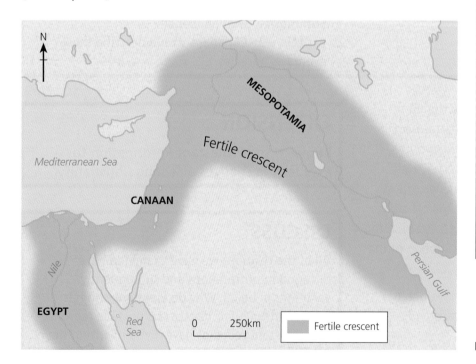

■ **Figure 5.20** The fertile crescent

Moses

1 I am the Lord thy god, who brought thee out of the land of Egypt, out of the house of **bondage**.
2 Thou shalt have no other gods before Me.
3 Thou shalt not take the name of the Lord thy God in vain.
4 Remember the Sabbath day to keep it holy.
5 Honor thy father and thy mother.
6 Thou **shalt** not murder
7 Thou shalt not commit adultery.
8 Thou shalt not steal.
9 Thou shalt not bear false witness against thy neighbor.
10 Thou shalt not **covet** anything that belongs to thy neighbor.

Note:
Bondage – Slavery
Shalt – Older version of the word shall
Covet – Take or steal

Source: www.jewishvirtuallibrary.org/jsource/Judaism/command.html

ACTIVITY: How does belief change over time?

■ ATL

Creative-thinking skills – Use brainstorming and visual diagrams to create new ideas and inquiries

It is often proposed that religions change with time and that this change is a response to external factors. In groups of four or five, **discuss** how you think the following factors might affect the development of religion and people's religious beliefs.

- **The experience of warfare or a natural disaster**
- **The movements of people around the world including contact with other religions**
- **New ideas and scientific discoveries**
- **Spiritual leaders who make claims about a particular religion**

Which other scenarios might affect belief systems?

REFLECTION

1 **Look at this quotation by George Carlin, a famous stand-up comedian of the twentieth century:**

   'Religion is like a pair of shoes … Find one that fits for you, but don't make me wear your shoes.'

   What do you think Carlin is saying in this quotation? Do you agree or disagree?
2 **The key concept for this chapter is systems. From looking at these religions, why do you think religion can be described as a system?**

According to Judaism, there were a number of covenants between Abraham's descendants and God. One example of this can be seen in the life of Moses, whose covenant forms an important part of the Jewish faith. Moses led the Jewish people from enslavement in Egypt back to Canaan over many years. This migration involved challenges and miracles. One of the major obstacles was overcoming ten plagues that were sent to stop the Jewish people from returning to Canaan: these included locusts, frogs, storms and boils on the skin.

Before they reached Canaan, Moses was given a covenant with God on Mount Sinai, which included the laws on which large sections of the Jewish faith are based. Within these laws were the Ten Commandments, inscribed on a stone tablet and kept in the 'Ark of the Covenant'. These laws were recorded in the **Torah** and provide guidance for Jews on how to live their life. The escape from slavery in Egypt is celebrated by Jews every year in the **Passover**, a religious festival.

Jewish worship takes place in the **synagogue**. **Rabbis** provide spiritual guidance in the religion; the religious texts include the Torah and the Talmud. Within the faith there is a major focus on ethical actions.

What is indigenous belief?

The indigenous people of the world possess an immense knowledge of their environments, based on centuries of living close to nature. Living in and from the richness and variety of complex ecosystems, they have an understanding of the properties of plants and animals, the functioning of ecosystems and the techniques for using and managing them that is particular and often detailed. In rural communities in developing countries, locally occurring species are relied on for many – sometimes all – foods, medicines, fuel, building materials and other products. Equally, people's knowledge and perceptions of the environment, and their relationships with it, are often important elements of cultural identity.

Frederico Mayor, Director General of UNESCO

Indigenous people are people who have occupied a particular area or territory since records began. These people tend to have very strong connections with the natural world and often have unique belief systems that guide their way of life.

There are thousands of different indigenous groups around the world, holding a wide range of beliefs. As these beliefs are often ancient, they can also provide an insight into how people lived thousands of years ago.

EXAMPLES OF INDIGENOUS GROUPS

The Ainu people

The Ainu are an indigenous group who are mainly from Hokkaido in northern Japan. They have an animist belief system: they believe that all living things have a 'Kamuy' inside them, which is a spirit. Animism is the belief that there is a spirit inside all living things. This includes plants, trees, all animals and even rocks. Ainu worship also includes reverence for the bear, which is seen as a very special animal because it provides them with a hide to keep warm in the winter and meat for food throughout the year. Their belief system involves a close relationship with nature and they have a hunter-gatherer lifestyle.

Only recently have the Ainu people been officially recognized as an indigenous group, and their numbers have diminished significantly over the years. It is now thought that only a handful of people in the world speak the Ainu language and it is classified as an endangered language.

■ **Figure 5.21** Ainu people in 1909

The Tuareg people

The Tuareg are an indigenous group from the Sahara region of Africa, including the countries of Mali, Niger and Algeria. They live a nomadic lifestyle, which means they move from place to place regularly, living in specially designed tents. They have a distinct language and cultural identity including music, food and clothing.

The Tuareg people adopted Islam as their religion and this influences their beliefs and practices.

The Tlinglit people

The Tlinglit are an indigenous tribe from North America, specifically from the Pacific Northwest of Canada. Also holding animist belief systems, their traditions include the use of shamans and totem poles.

Shamans are individuals within a particular community or tribe who represent a connection with the spirit world and are the healers and protectors in the group. Totems, most commonly associated with totem poles, are often used to represent stories relevant to the particular culture and contain the faces of animals or birds. Native American tribes often make use of totem poles as part of their cultural identity and belief.

The Awá people

The Awá are an indigenous tribe from the Amazon rainforests of Brazil and they are a severely threatened group. The threats to their lifestyle and existence have come as a result of deforestation.

Recently, the Brazilian government has recognized the land rights of this group but their numbers are so low that their future is not certain. The Awá live such a remote lifestyle that it is thought there are still a number of them who have not had contact with the outside world. There are many threatened tribes in the Amazon region of South America.

What examples are there of non-religious belief?

We have discussed examples of religious and indigenous belief, but belief is not always connected to a particular religion or cultural identity. Non-religious belief is common in the world today. For instance, one belief that has a large number of followers is that of **atheism**. Atheists directly challenge religious belief and also question its value as they often believe that it creates many problems for people. Famous thinkers and writers about atheism include evolutionary biologist Richard Dawkins and author Christopher Hitchins.

Agnostics on the other hand believe that it is not possible to know whether a God exists or not. Consequently, they do not reject religion but do not accept it either.

Another group, **humanists**, believe in the importance of living a fulfilled life. Humanism has its origins during the Renaissance, which took place from the late fourteenth century through to the eighteenth century in Europe. Humanists challenged many of the religious teachings about the weaknesses of humans and emphasized the importance of enjoying life but also critical thinking and reasoning. This had a cultural impact on the arts as the importance of human achievement and life were celebrated, often challenging many of the religious traditions at the time.

Nowadays, humanism continues to have a following as many people look for non-religious answers to some of the big questions they have about themselves and the world.

> ## DISCUSS
>
> Read through the quotations in Figure 5.22.
>
> 1 **Summarize** the different viewpoints presented here.
> 2 **In groups of four, discuss and debate the following question: 'Is it possible to believe in nothing?'**

What can be asserted without proof can be dismissed without proof.

Christopher Hitchins

I am against religion because it teaches us to be satisfied with not understanding the world.

Richard Dawkins

If you're an atheist, you know, you believe, this is the only life you're going to get. It's a precious life. It's a beautiful life. It's something we should live to the full, to the end of our days. Where if you're religious and you believe in another life somehow, that means you don't live this life to the full because you think you're going to get another one. That's an awfully negative way to live a life. Being an atheist frees you up to live this life properly, happily and fully.

Richard Dawkins

■ **Figure 5.22**

! Take action

! Host a web chat with students from a different school where they might hold a different perspective on belief to your own. You could look at the 'Face to Faith' online learning community to help you to do this: **www.facetofaithonline.org**

! **Explore** the work of Survival International and their campaigns to protect indigenous people: **www.survivalinternational.org**

SUMMATIVE ASSESSMENT TASK: Written essay on belief

■ ATL

- Communication skills – Structure information in summaries, essays and reports
- Critical-thinking skills – Gather and organize relevant information to formulate an argument

Write a 500–700 word essay response to the following research question:

'Discuss the different ways that belief can affect people's lives.'

The command term for this task is highlighted below.

Discuss – Offer a considered and balanced review that includes a range of arguments, factors or hypotheses. Opinions or conclusions should be presented clearly and supported by evidence.

Definition from IB MYP Individuals and societies guide, *2014*

Suggested steps for completing the task

1 Brainstorm ideas, examples and arguments that you could use in your answer. At this stage just think of as many things as possible.
2 Create an action plan, showing your organization, research and planning as you prepare to write your essay. This will be assessed against Criterion B (see action plan advice section below).
3 Write a plan for your answer. What information will you include in your introduction, body paragraphs and conclusion?
4 Submit your essay to your teacher; make sure you include a bibliography. Check your work thoroughly before submission.

◆ Assessment opportunities:

This activity can be assessed using Criterion A: Knowing and understanding (strands i and ii), Criterion B: Investigating (strands ii and iii) and Criterion C: Communicating (strands i, ii and iii).

Action plan advice

Action plans are designed to help you to create a better quality end product. You use them throughout the task. Action plans will vary depending on the task you are working on but the following areas are helpful to work on in your action plan.

1 **Organization** – This should detail your time frame for completing the work: a checklist of tasks that need to be completed and when you intend to complete them.

2 **Research** – This should include any research that you have conducted in the preparation of your assessment. You should always keep a record of the sources used in this process.

3 **Planning** – This section should include information on how you will structure and communicate your assessment. In this case, it will be the planning of your essay answer.

Reflection

This chapter has explored different examples of belief systems and how they affect people. Different belief systems can be seen to have an impact on people's identity by providing guidance on lifestyle, rituals and different practices.

Use this table to reflect on your own learning in this chapter		
Questions we asked	Answers we found	Any further questions now?
Factual What are the beliefs of the major world religions? What is indigenous belief? What examples are there of non-religious belief?		
Conceptual How does belief change over time? How can identity be shaped by personal belief?		
Debatable To what extent does belief cloud or clarify our judgement? Is it possible to believe in nothing?		

		How well did you master the skills?			
Approaches to learning you used in this chapter	Description – what new skills did you learn?	Novice	Learner	Practitioner	Expert
Communication skills					
Creative-thinking skills					
Critical-thinking skills					
Information literacy skills					
Transfer skills					

Learner profile attribute(s)	Reflect on the importance of open-mindedness for your learning in this chapter.
Open-minded	

6 What factors contribute to the fairness and development of societies?

○ Access to **resources** and **equality** of opportunities can help societies to **develop** to become **fairer** places but this is often dependent on **global interactions**.

CONSIDER THESE QUESTIONS:

Factual: What is poverty? What is development and how do we measure it? How can resources help to reduce extreme poverty? What is aid?

Conceptual: What factors influence the development of a country?

Debatable: What do we need? Is there a connection between health and wealth?

Now **share and compare** your thoughts and ideas with your partner, or with the whole class.

■ **Figure 6.1** A homeless man holding money

○ IN THIS CHAPTER, WE WILL …

■ **Find out** about poverty in the world and its consequences.
■ **Explore** the factors that contribute to the development of a country.
■ **Take action** by reflecting and acting on issues in our local communities.

KEY WORDS

absolute poverty	needs
aid	poverty line
consumerism	poverty trap
development	relative poverty
Human Development Index	resources
	wants

Sidewalk Bubblegum ©1996 Clay Butler

■ Figure 6.2 A cartoon commenting on consumer culture

For many people, living in the twenty-first century provides a huge array of choices and opportunities. From the latest computer games to different brands of shoes, there is a constant flow of options for people to spend money on. This is **consumerism**, and we see it in shopping malls across the world and online with internet shopping. But have you ever stopped and thought about how necessary it all is?

What do we need?

What do we actually need?

This type of thinking can be divided into the categories of **wants** and **needs**. Wants are the things we might desire to make our life more enjoyable while needs are the things that are essential to our life. Look at this list and think about which things you would consider to be wants and which things you would consider to be needs:

- air to breathe
- shelter
- chocolate
- clothes
- water
- access to health care.

From the list we should see that they are all examples of needs except for chocolate. We need air to breathe, we need water to drink; we also need food but this does not have to be chocolate. Wants are things that we would like to have but they are not essential.

In the twentieth century an American psychologist called Abraham Maslow created a theory to demonstrate what people need to lead a fulfilled life. This is known as Maslow's hierarchy of needs.

Maslow suggests that we begin with more basic physical needs such as breathing and eating and move on to more complex needs such as the need to belong, to have positive self-esteem and, finally, to achieve self-actualization. Self-actualization means to understand one's potential and interests and to work towards fulfilling them: for instance, becoming an artist, or working to help others in need.

Unfortunately, many people in the world are unable to meet their needs and this is often due to the circumstances and environment that they live in. In this chapter we will explore how being in poverty can affect people negatively and look at the causes and consequences. We will also look at how countries develop and the challenges and opportunities associated with this.

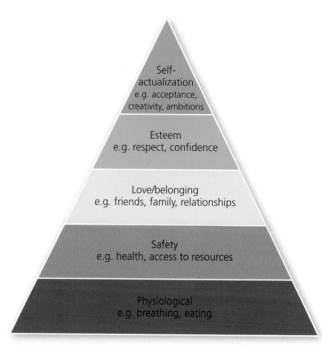

■ **Figure 6.3** Maslow's hierarchy of needs

DISCUSS

What could you do if you had US$1 per day to live on? Think about the needs and wants in your own life.

What is poverty?

Poverty means to be very poor. This often refers to a lack of material possessions or money to buy the basic necessities but can also involve a lack of access to resources, freedoms and services that help people to avoid poverty. A lot of progress has been made in the twenty-first century to reduce poverty but it is still a major global issue.

There are two major types of poverty: **absolute poverty** and **relative poverty**. Absolute is the worst type of poverty and it is also referred to as extreme poverty. It refers to the condition of not having the means to meet the basic needs such as food, shelter and health care. Definitions vary but people living in absolute poverty often have as little as US$1 per day on which to live. Absolute poverty tends to occur in locations where people do not have access to resources or are disadvantaged due to a variety of factors outside of their control.

The second type of poverty is relative poverty. This is characterized by people being poor in comparison to others in a particular society. This is a common form of poverty as social inequality exists throughout the world. Relative poverty occurs in both economically rich and poor countries; however, the severity of relative poverty can be reduced by the actions and policies of governments on behalf of their people. Relative poverty can also be seen in ways not directly related to money as shown in Table 6.1.

■ **Table 6.1** Types of poverty

Types of poverty	Characteristics
Educational	People have limited access to schooling – this can lead to illiteracy.
Economic	This refers to a lack of money to buy essential items – the income of the household is not sufficient.
Social and political	This happens when people are isolated or excluded from a particular society. For example, an immigrant living in a country without rights to work, or people experiencing prejudice based on a disability or their race or gender.
Health	This is a form of poverty that occurs when people do not have access to proper health facilities such as vaccinations, hospitals and doctors.
Safety and security	This is a type of poverty where people do not feel safe – this might be to do with exposure to violence within a home or living in an environment with high levels of crime. The outbreak of a war also creates these conditions.

■ **Figure 6.4** Poverty in the Great Depression in the USA in the 1930s

ACTIVITY: Types of poverty

■ ATL

Communication skills – Use a variety of speaking techniques to communicate with a variety of audiences

Create a role play to illustrate one example of a type of poverty that people might experience. Be creative with your ideas and then perform the role play in front of the class to see if they can correctly **identify** the example.

COLOUR–SYMBOL–IMAGE

Choose one colour, one symbol and one image to represent poverty based on the work you have done on it so far. **Discuss** in groups the reasons why you made these choices.

CASE STUDY – POVERTY IN THE USA

Despite being one of the wealthiest nations in the world, the USA has a high number of people living in relative poverty. The USA (as well as many other countries) uses a measure called the **poverty line** to describe the minimum income needed for a family to support itself. In 2015, if a family of four in the USA had an annual income of less than approximately US$23,000 then they were classified as poor and living below the poverty line.

SOURCE A

■ **Figure 6.5** A man dragging his possessions past homeless people in Los Angeles, California

SOURCE B

Sharon Dory in Mendocino County, California

'For seven years, I lived on $500 a month. The cost of taxes on my small home was more than $200 monthly. Volunteering was the only "recreation" I could afford. I feel rich when I have food.'

SOURCE C

Tania Parsons

'I'm a single mom and I make under $11,000 a year. The only way to do well for us is with food stamps. Without it, we couldn't eat. The government reduced the amount we get so by the end of the month we ran out of milk, juices, bread, eggs. It's difficult when one child is only three. They have health insurance, but I was told I don't qualify for it. In my area, rent is high and all of my income goes to it. I don't want to become homeless again. It's scary.'

SOURCE D

George Leake in Vallejo, California

'I've lived below the poverty line for years now. There's a number of things you can do to make it: don't own a car, try to grow your own food, cook everything from scratch, don't buy anything unless you absolutely need it, couch surf with friends, barter rent for yard work, cleaning or other services, try to shop at thrift stores or garage sales. Last year, I found a pair of shoes my size that were getting thrown away. The threads started coming off, so I fixed them with shoe glue: they were much better shoes than the cheapest ones you can find which only last a month at most. I know so many people living like this. The idea of having things like cable TV, cell phones or iPads is so ridiculous – many of us read books from the library for entertainment.'

Statistics showing the percentage of people in the USA living below the poverty line. (Data from US Census Bureau)

Year	2002	2003	2004	2005	2006	2007	2008	2009	2010	2011	2012	2013
%	12.1	12.5	12.7	12.6	12.3	12.5	13.2	14.3	15.1	15.	15.	14.5

ACTIVITY: Poverty in the USA

 ATL

Information literacy skills – Access information to be informed and to inform others; Process data and report results

1   **What is the difference between relative poverty and absolute poverty?**
2   **Copy and complete the following table.**

Person	What can you learn about poverty from their story?	What else would you like to know?
Sharon		
Tania		
George		

3   **Using the data in Source E, construct a line graph (similar to Figure 6.6) to represent the data.**

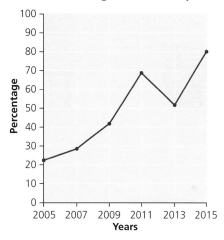

■ **Figure 6.6** Example line graph

4   **Using the information on your graph, write down three statements to describe what it shows.**

Line graphs

Line graphs are useful in humanities for representing data that show change over time. They use an *x*-axis (horizontal) and a *y*-axis (vertical). Points are plotted on the line graph and then connected together with a series of straight lines. The *x*-axis is usually used to display the time period (for example, a particular year or month) and the *y*-axis would show the thing being measured (for example, crime rates or unemployment figures).

Learning to construct line graphs is a useful skill and you should aim to complete the graph to a high standard of presentation.

THE POVERTY TRAP

One of the biggest problems with poverty is trying to find solutions to get people out of poverty. An economic theory, the **poverty trap**, suggests that owing to a variety of factors, families can be trapped in poverty for several generations.

■ **Figure 6.7** The poverty trap

REFLECTION

■ ATL

Reflection skills – Consider content

Copy and complete the table.

LIST – Reasons why people get stuck in the poverty trap	REFLECT – Possible solutions to weaken/end the poverty trap for people

DISCUSS

'People can escape poverty if they have a job.' Do you agree?

What is development and how do we measure it?

DEVELOPMENT

Poverty occurs in all countries. However, poorer countries can be more likely to have absolute poverty. Countries are often ranked due to their level of development and they can be described as either developed or developing. This refers to whether they have reached a certain level of economic and human development. **Economic development** refers to the wealth of a country and **human development** refers to the quality of life for people living in the particular country.

Developed countries tend to run effectively, have good infrastructure (such as roads and public transport), good quality education and health facilities. They also tend to have relatively high levels of income for the people living there.

Developing countries may have strong aspects such as high income levels or good quality education but may fall down in other areas. Some developing countries may have very poor resources and services for the people living there.

It is important to remember that labelling a country as either developed or developing can be misleading as there are a number of factors at play. Also, there are significant differences within each category. For example, two developed countries may have very notable differences in the quality of their education provision, while two developing countries may have a large difference in terms of the average life expectancy.

Table 6.2 lists some of the ways that countries are measured in terms of their development.

■ **Table 6.2** Ways to measure development

Examples of ways to measure economic development	Examples of ways to measure human development
Gross Domestic Product (GDP)	Quality of health care
Gross National Income (GNI)	Quality of education
Wealth inequality	Life expectancy
Unemployment rate	Gender equality
Economic growth	Literacy rate

MEASURING DEVELOPMENT

As there are so many ways to measure development this leads to a range of perspectives on what constitutes a developed country. In addition, the pace of change that occurs around the world means that it is difficult to make generalizations about levels of development as it can change quickly.

One measure that has grown in popularity in recent years is that of the Human Development Index (HDI), which is used by the United Nations. This is a measure of a combination of economic and human development indicators including life expectancy, education and income. The figure used to measure a country varies between 0 and 1, with 1 being the highest possible score.

The graph in Figure 6.8 shows the ten highest scoring countries in 2015.

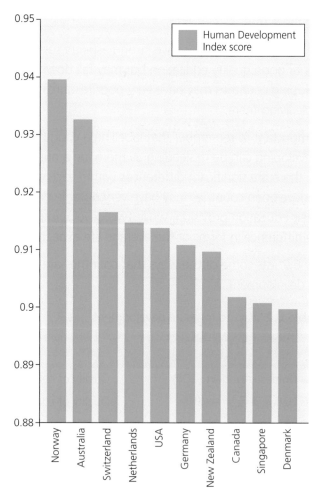

EXTENSION

Choose a country from Figure 6.8 to research. Think about the reasons why it reached a high score in the Human Development Index. Compare your findings with those of other members of your class.

■ **Figure 6.8** Human Development Index score – ten highest countries in 2015

What factors influence the development of a country?

■ **Table 6.3** Factors influencing the development of a country

Geographic	Historical	Political	Economic
Geographic factors are linked to location and climate of a particular country. These have an influence on a country's ability to develop as its location can create a range of natural advantages or disadvantages. For example, locations with very high levels of sunshine and very little rain would have problems with the development of farming, or countries that experience regular earthquakes owing to their location can have development problems.	Historical factors are important for understanding how countries develop over time. Wars that occurred in the past often have long-term consequences that would affect development. If one country is taken over by another this can have an impact on its development; for example, colonialism.	Corrupt governments hold back the development of a country by wasting money or keeping it for themselves. Governments need to run countries effectively in order for development to benefit people in society.	The health of the economy of a country is vitally important to its development. Countries that develop positive trading relationships with other countries and have good economic investment in infrastructure, business, industry, agriculture, education and health tend to develop well. Countries can develop in uneven patterns; for example, cities may have better quality resources and infrastructure compared to rural areas.

ACTIVITY: Factors that influence development

■ ATL

Critical-thinking skills – Draw reasonable conclusions and generalizations

Read the following statements and **identify** the ways that each example could affect the development of a country. **Discuss** your ideas in groups.

1 **This country has a temperate climate; this means that it is never too hot or too cold throughout the year.**
2 **This country shares borders with other countries that have good levels of development.**
3 **This country is run by a dictator whose family is the richest in the whole country.**
4 **This country has invested a lot of money in education.**
5 **This country has vast reserves of natural resources.**

EXTENSION

The resource curse

There are many countries in the world that have an abundance of natural resources but have not developed well either economically or in terms of human development. This pattern is sometimes described as the **resource curse**. This suggests that rather than aiding the development of a country, an abundance of natural resources such as oil, gold or diamonds can actually hold back the development of a country. This is explained through countries overly depending on their resources in an uneven manner, or through the exploitation of these resources in an unsustainable way or with corruption. This can also be linked to international competition for resources that does not consider the development of the country.

The resource curse has often been linked to the problems associated with development of the Democratic Republic of Congo in Africa. Look at this article to research this issue in more detail. **www.bbc.com/news/magazine-24396390**

Is there a connection between health and wealth?

REFLECTION

What do you think are the main challenges associated with measuring the development of a country?

When studying development, it seems a fair conclusion to make that if a country is wealthy then surely the health of the people living there will improve. Look at Table 6.4 for the year 2013.

■ **Table 6.4** Average life expectancy and income per person, 2013

Country	Costa Rica	Norway	Central African Republic	Japan	France	Somalia	India	Equatorial Guinea	Russia
Life expectancy	80	81	53	83	82	58	66	59	71
Income per person in US dollars	13,430	63,320	584	35,610	37,310	619	5,244	32,650	23,560

ACTIVITY: The connection between health and wealth

■ ATL

- Information literacy skills – Access information to be informed and to inform others

Table 6.4 shows a **cross section** (selection) of countries in the world with their average life expectancy and income per person.

1 Using the data, do you think there is a connection between health and wealth? **Explain** your answer with examples.
2 Are there any significant anomalies (exceptions)? Do some research into these countries to find out reasons for their results.
3 Go to the Gapminder website:

  www.gapminder.org/tools/bubbles

  Spend some time exploring the 'Health & Wealth of Nations' chart to **investigate** these issues further.

▼ Links to: Physical and health education

Differing perspectives on development – Bhutan and Gross National Happiness

The country of Bhutan in Asia has criticized the use of measuring the development of a country based on the economic wealth of the people who live there. In 1972, the King of Bhutan proposed the measure of 'Gross National Happiness' to determine whether a country is developed or not.

Bhutan is a relatively isolated country in the Himalayas that places a major emphasis on Buddhist teachings and living in harmony with the natural environment.

The Gross National Happiness scale places emphasis on the well-being of people and is observed through various measures such as their psychological health, quality of education, the natural environment and living conditions.

Bhutan represents an interesting case study of a country that takes a different view on the idea of what being developed actually means.

Discuss: What do you think? Is the well-being of the people more important than their economic wealth? Can you make connections to your studies of physical and health education?

■ **Figure 6.9** Monks in Bhutan

ACTIVITY: Development profile

For this task you need to create a profile of a country of your choice. You need to **investigate** and **explore** different aspects of the country and come to a final decision on how developed you think it is.

There are many websites where you can find data to help you to complete this task but the following could be particularly useful:

- www.cia.gov/library/publications/the-world-factbook
- http://data.worldbank.org
- www.gapminder.org

You should **reflect** on the relative strengths and weaknesses of your chosen country. Within your profile you could also include a location map and supporting images and graphs.

Table 6.5 could be used to help you to reach a decision about the development of the country.

You will need to provide a list of the sources you used in your research for this task as well as a reflection on the research process and results.

■ **Table 6.5**

Development indicator	Strengths	Weaknesses
SOCIAL (examples include quality of education, health care provision, life expectancy, literacy rates)		
ECONOMIC (examples include GDP, GNI, income levels for people, unemployment figures, trade relations)		
POLITICAL (examples include levels of freedom/censorship, political rights, international relations)		
ENVIRONMENTAL (examples include sustainability, pollution levels, environmental quality)		

◆ Assessment opportunities:

This activity can be assessed using Criterion A: Knowing and understanding (strands i and ii), Criterion B: Investigating (strand iv) and Criterion C: Communicating (strands i, ii and iii).

How can resources help to reduce extreme poverty?

The idea that some lives matter less is the root of all that's wrong with the world.

Dr Paul Farmer

To get away from poverty, you need several things at the same time: school, health, and infrastructure – those are the public investments. And on the other side, you need market opportunities, information, employment, and human rights.

Dr Hans Rosling

The steps that are needed from the developed nations are clear. The first is ensuring trade justice. I have said before that trade justice is a truly meaningful way for the developed countries to show commitment to bringing about an end to global poverty. The second is an end to the debt crisis for the poorest countries. The third is to deliver much more aid and make sure it is of the highest quality.

Nelson Mandela

■ **Figure 6.10**

DISCUSS

Look at the quotations in Figure 6.10. What suggestions are being made about the ways that extreme poverty can be reduced in the world?

ACTIVITY: Diamond 9

■ ATL

Critical-thinking skills – Propose and evaluate a variety of solutions

In groups, create your own diamond 9 of the cards in Figure 6.12. Rearrange the cards in order of importance. The cards at the top would be what you consider to be the most important solutions while those lower down would be of lesser priority. **Discuss** your ideas in your group.

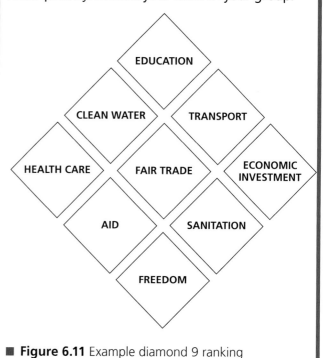

■ **Figure 6.11** Example diamond 9 ranking

HEALTH CARE
Access to medicines, doctors and hospitals is vitally important. If sickness is left untreated or people do not have the vaccines they need, they are being disadvantaged from the outset.

ACCESS TO CLEAN WATER
Water is essential but many people have to walk miles to their nearest source of clean water. By having to spend this time walking they are unable to earn money to improve their living conditions. Clean water sources also improve health.

ECONOMIC INVESTMENT
People need jobs and the opportunity to create businesses. Government investment allows for economic growth to create jobs and to provide money for people starting their own business. People living in poverty often need loans so that they can use the money to create a business. Workers also need fair pay and to not be exploited.

FAIR TRADING REGULATIONS
Farmers who produce crops that are sold to other countries sometimes do not receive fair pay for their work. Through better regulation and the commitment of distribution and processing companies this can improve.

SANITATION
Sanitation means to have a clean place to live with working toilets and sewer systems. Without good sanitation, diseases spread easily. For example, cholera is a very serious disease that results from dirty water.

AID
Aid comes in many forms to people who need it the most. In times of crisis such as war, famine and drought, aid agencies provide the essential items to people in need. These are often things such as clean water, medical aid, food and shelter. Other forms of aid can be for more long-term development; for instance, aid that helps to develop infrastructure (for example, schools, roads and hospitals).

EDUCATION
Education allows people to learn to read and write, develop numeracy skills and develop their different strengths. Without education it is difficult for people to gain jobs to lift themselves out of poverty. Education does not just refer to schools; it also includes universities, libraries and museums.

TRANSPORT
Mobility is really important to escaping poverty. Cheap and readily available public transport allows people to get to school or get to their job thus improving their chances of escaping poverty. There have been campaigns by many charities recently to provide far more readily available access to bicycles for people who have no means of transport.

POLITICAL AND SOCIAL FREEDOMS
Without freedom of speech and movement it is difficult for people to change their conditions. Repressive governments hold back people's ability to escape poverty and at times can actually create worse conditions for poverty to thrive.

■ **Figure 6.12** Ways in which poverty can be reduced

CASE STUDY – FAIRTRADE

You may have seen the Fairtrade Foundation logo on different items in supermarkets. The movement was started to promote better trading conditions for people in developing countries who may have, in the past, been exploited by unfair trading regulations.

DISCUSS

According to Sources A and B, what have been the benefits of the Fairtrade movement to these farmers?

Reflect upon the ways that different global interactions can have a positive impact on the development of different countries.

■ **Figure 6.13** Red coffee beans grown on a Fairtrade coffee farm

SOURCE A

Gerardo Arias Camacho, coffee producer, Costa Rica

'In the 1980s, the price of coffee fell so low that it didn't cover the cost of production. Many farmers abandoned their land and went to the cities to find work. Some even left the country. In the mid-90s, I decided to go to America to make money and support my family. After eight years, I had earned enough to buy the family farm so that my parents could retire. But coffee prices were still so low that I was forced to go back to the States for another two years.

'The coffee market was so unstable. We did not have a local school, good roads or bridges. Now that our consortium is Fairtrade-certified, prices are stable and we receive a guaranteed premium. We spend the money on education, environmental protection, roads and bridges, and improving the old processing plant. We have sponsored a scholarship programme so that our kids can stay in school.

'I believe that my cooperative would be out of business if it wasn't for Fairtrade. Free trade is not responsible trade. When prices go down, farmers produce more and prices drop further. Fairtrade is the way trade should be: fair, responsible and sustainable.

'My oldest son is in college, my ten-year-old has already had as much education as me, and my little princess is in her second year at school. With the help of Fairtrade, they might all be able to go to university and get a degree. They won't have to jump the border from Mexico to America, leaving their country for ten years, like me. They can decide what they want in life. I tell them: "You have two choices. You can be a coffee grower or you can be something else. But learn how to be a coffee grower first, like your father and your grandfather."'

SOURCE B

Makandianfing Keita, cotton farmer, Mali

'Cotton prices were going down and down until they were below the cost of production. People were demotivated and it was very depressing. But now, we can make a sustainable living. My family can eat and we have better health.

'In the past, children had to walk 10 km to go to school, so really it was impossible. We have now been able to build a school. At first it had two classrooms. When we had more money and wanted to expand, we challenged the government to match our investment. Now there are five classrooms in total, and every child in the village can go to school.

'Pregnant women had no access to healthcare. Many died in childbirth and there were high rates of infant mortality. Now we have built a maternity centre. We have also built a food storage facility so that we can have a year-round food supply, and we have installed a pump for drinking water. We have built a new road, enabling us to travel further than 5 km outside of the village without difficulty.

'Fairtrade standards called for better agricultural practices. Before, empty pesticide containers would be used as water carriers. In some cases this led to death. Now, we dispose of waste properly. We don't burn bushes any more, we prevent soil erosion and we have effective irrigation.'

What is aid?

AID

Aid refers to the supply of resources to communities in need of help for a range of reasons.

Aid is often sent as a rapid response to a specific event that might occur in a country. This includes war, famine, drought and natural disasters such as floods and earthquakes. This is known as short-term aid and often involves the delivery of essential supplies including water, food and medicines.

Other forms of aid occur on long-term projects such as building infrastructure and services in countries, training people with specific skills and working with governments. A number of charities work on a specific issue and use their funds to support the locations where this issue is severe.

SUMMATIVE ASSESSMENT TASK: Development plan

■ ATL

- Critical-thinking skills – Consider ideas from multiple perspectives; Gather and organize relevant information to formulate an argument
- Creative-thinking skills – Create novel solutions to authentic problems

You work for an international agency that specializes in development. Your organization provides recommendations to countries on how to find solutions to poverty and development problems. You have been given the following case to look at.

The country you have been given to look at has experienced war for the past five years. Peace has now arrived and people are keen to move their lives forward and improve conditions within the country. War has created a number of problems. The infrastructure of the country has been damaged so there is a lack of good roads, schools and hospitals. People have limited access to clean water for drinking. Land here is very fertile and many crops can be grown easily but war has led to a number of landmines being left in rural areas, which if stepped on can lead to injury or death. The country has a number of natural advantages, including a coastline and significant natural resources, such as copper, that can be mined and then sold internationally.

Since the war there is a new government in power, which wants to work with your agency and would be interested in listening to your suggestions.

Your task is to write a plan for the government with three short-term goals and three long-term goals to help the development of the country. You should aim to make the plan between 400 and 600 words in length. Structure the plan with subheadings and explanations of each of the goals and what you hope they would achieve.

You need to make sure that you consider the perspectives of the following groups of people within your plan:

- **Farmers** – They are able to work the land very effectively but need help to avoid the dangerous landmines and with the distribution of their produce to the market.
- **Children** – Education is in a bad state due to war: there are not enough schools and teachers; illiteracy rates are increasing.
- **Government** – The government's biggest concern is the availability of clean water; it would be happy to accept aid to help with this.
- **Doctors and nurses** – Owing to large amounts of investment before the war, there is a sufficient number of doctors and nurses in the country. But many are choosing to work in other countries because of the lack of facilities and poor working conditions.
- **Miners** – Mining is a big part of the economy of the country but often in the past, miners have been underpaid for their work. The government now controls all of the mines.

Your agency also works closely with two aid agencies that can offer relief to some of the problems. The first, 'Emergency Aid', is able to help with the distribution of water, medicines and vaccinations, clearing landmines and the building of roads. The second, 'Sustainable Futures', specializes in the development of industry and education. It works with governments in a long-term relationship to develop services, systems and infrastructure over time.

When you have completed your plan, complete a reflection. Think about what went well in your work and how you might do things differently next time.

◆ Assessment opportunities:

This activity can be assessed using Criterion A: Knowing and understanding (strand ii), Criterion C: Communicating (strands i and ii) and Criterion D: Thinking critically (strands ii and iv).

Reflection

In this chapter we have explored the issue of poverty and how it affects people throughout the world. We have reflected and inquired into how countries develop and some of the solutions to improving the fairness and development of different societies.

Use this table to reflect on your own learning in this chapter		
Questions we asked	Answers we found	Any further questions now?
Factual What is poverty? What is development and how do we measure it? How can resources help to reduce extreme poverty? What is aid?		
Conceptual What factors influence the development of a country?		
Debatable What do we need? Is there a connection between health and wealth?		

Approaches to learning you used in this chapter	Description – what new skills did you learn?	How well did you master the skills?			
		Novice	Learner	Practitioner	Expert
Communication skills					
Creative-thinking skills					
Critical-thinking skills					
Information literacy skills					

Learner profile attribute(s)	Reflect on the importance of being a thinker for your learning in this chapter.
Thinker	

Glossary

absolute poverty   The state of being extremely poor with little to no resources to help you out of the situation

agnostic   Belief that it is impossible to know whether a God exists or not

aid   The provision of goods or services to help out people in need

apostles   12 followers of Jesus Christ

atheism   Belief that there is no God

belief   Something that is thought to be true with conviction

birth rate   The number of births per thousand people of a population

cardinal points   The points on a compass – North, East, South, West

cartography   The study of maps

contour lines   Lines on a map showing areas of equal height

contour interval   Distance between contour lines

civilization   An advanced society

city   A large settlement

conurbations   Extended urban area, merging of different towns

covenant   An agreement between God and his people, important to the Jewish faith

consumerism   The process of advertising and selling goods that people might want to buy for themselves

deforestation   The process of cutting down trees and not replanting them; leading to a reduced number of trees in the world

dharma   Moral duties for Hindus

disciples   Followers of Jesus Christ

denomination   A branch of a particular religion

function   The main industry or role of a settlement e.g. fishing

grid references   Either a four figure or six figure number that provides a location point on a map

governance   Refers to the different ways of ruling a society e.g. monarchy

gold rush   Historical time period in the 19th century when many people went to find gold in the west of the USA

green belt   Area that is protected from urban development

human rights   Term used for the rights that people expect to have worldwide; for example, the right to life and the right to work

hieroglyphics   System of writing developed in Ancient Egypt

humanists   During the Renaissance these people sought to explore the capabilities of human action and creativity

Human Development Index   A measurement of the economic and social well being of people within a country

irrigation   Technique in farming for moving water around to help with the growing of crops

karma   Peoples' actions in one life determines what will happen in future lives

moksha   Path to escape the cycle of birth, life and death

megacities   Cities of over 10 million people

meditation   The act of thinking deeply with focus for a certain period of time

nirvana   Buddhist term for reaching enlightenment

needs   Things that are essential to life e.g. water

Passover   Jewish religious festival

pollution   Damaging the environment by the disposal or release of harmful materials

philosophy   The study of knowledge and human existence

public health   Health facilities provided for all the people by a government

primary sources   Sources that are from the time e.g. a coin, letter or newspaper

push and pull factors   Factors that make people either leave (push) or be attracted (pull) to move to a different location

pilgrimage   A journey to a special place that holds significance

prayer   A spoken act of worship

poverty line   The point at which it is possible to live a life without needing help from others, living below the line means to be living in poverty

poverty trap   Situation where the same communities stay trapped in poverty due to circumstances out of their control

rabbi   Religious leader within Judaism

recycling   Converting something back into a usable product e.g. recycled paper

reincarnation   Cycle of life and death, being reborn after death

relief   Variation in the height of an area of terrain

relative poverty   The state of being poor in comparison to others, less extreme than absolute poverty

Reformation   Historic time period when the religious teachings of Christianity were challenged, leading to the creation of new denominations within the religion

resources   Materials and goods that are required

ritual   Series of actions or traditions associated with a religion

rural   Area within the countryside

samsara – Buddhist term for the cycle of birth, life and death

scale   On a map, scale represents the distance in real life

secondary sources   Sources that are produced at a later date to the event in question e.g. books

site   Location for a settlement

sphere of influence   Areas that a settlement has influence over

situation   The position of a settlement, location and surroundings

settlement   A place where people live e.g town or city

sustainability   Methods used to ensure something will last into the future; for example, environmentally friendly policies by a government

synagogue   A place of worship for Jews

topographic   Showing the different physical features accurately

Torah   Religious text of Judaism

trinity   How God appears according to Christianity as the father, son and Holy Spirit

urban   Areas within cities and towns

Vedas   Sacred writings of Hinduism

water cycle   The movement of water around the planet

wants   Non-essential things that people may want to have e.g. a new car

Acknowledgements

The Publishers would like to thank the following for permission to reproduce copyright material. Every effort has been made to trace all copyright holders, but if any have been inadvertently overlooked the Publishers will be pleased to make the necessary arrangements at the first opportunity.

Photo credits

p.2 © Andrew Aitchison/Alamy Stock Photo; **p.3** *l* © Per Anders Pettersson/AFP/Getty Images, *r* © Ashley Cooper/Getty Images; **p.4** *t* © timy1973/Thinkstock/iStockphoto/Getty Images, *m* © E+/ Getty Images, *b* © Huntstock/Thinkstock/Getty Images; **p.5** *t* © Only5/iStock/Thinkstock/Getty Images, *b* ©3DSculptor/iStock/Thinkstock/Getty Images; **p.9** © Steve Greenberg/CartoonStock.com; **p.10** © fergregory/iStock/Thinkstock/Getty Images; **p.11** © Adam Borkowski/Fotolia; **p.12** *b* © Ocean Conservancy; **p.14** © Reinhard Dirscherl/ullstein bild/Getty Images; **p.18** © Tatiana Edrenkina/123RF. com; **p.19** © Albachiaraa/iStock/Thinkstock/Getty Images; **p.20** *l* Courtesy of the Library of Congress, LC USZ62-117124, *m* © Eye Ubiquitous/Alamy Stock Photo, *r* © robertharding/Alamy Stock Photo, *b* © Peter Cavanagh/Alamy Stock Photo; **p.24** © Sustainable Development Knowledge Platform (http:// sustainabledevelopment.un.org); **p.28–9** © Tryfonov/Fotolia; **p.30** *tl* © Alex Livesey/FIFA/Contributor/ Getty Images, *bl* ©Lucian Milasan/123RF.com, *tr* From the LSE Library's collections, *br* © Stephen Walter; **p.32** *tl* ©PeterHermesFurian/iStock/Thinkstock/Getty Images, *tr* Reprinted with permission from Ordnance survey, *bl* Climate Classification of Australia, Bureau of Meteorology. Retrieved from https://www.researchgate.net/figure/274901906_fig2_Fig-2-Major-Australian-climatic-zones-Source-Bureau-of-Meteorology, *br* ©Blueberg/ Alamy Stock Photo; **p.33** *tl* ©Lucian Milasan/123RF. com, *bl* © FrankRamspott/iStockphoto.com, *r* © Gianluca D'Auri Muscelli/iStock/Thinkstock/Getty Images; **p.34** © Stripped Pixel/Fotolia; **p.38** © DanielPrudek/iStock/Thinkstock/Getty Images; **p.40** © Sandancer1088/iStock/Thinkstock/Getty Images; **p.41** Reprinted with permission from Ordnance survey; **p.48** © gionnixxx/iStock/Thinkstock/Getty Images; **p.50** © Rasiel Suarez; **p.51** *l* © Corbis, *r* © lapas77 – Fotolia; **p.54** © De Agostini Picture Library/De Agostini/Getty Images; **p.56** *l* © Jane Arraf/MCT/MCT/Getty Images, *r* © DeAgostini/Getty Images; **p.58** © Apic/Getty Images; **p.65** © gkrobar/iStock/Thinkstock/Getty Images; **p.68** *t* © Viacheslav Lopatin/123RF.com, *b* © Atlaspix/ Alamy Stock Photo; **p.73** © Jgz/Fotolia; **p.76** © Fred49/iStock/Thinkstock/Getty Images; **p.77** *l* © flocu/iStock/Thinkstock/Getty Images, *m* © YMZK-photo/Thinkstock/iStockphoto/Getty Images, *r* © KeepYourEyesWideOpen//Thinkstock/iStockphoto/Getty Images; **p.78** © Henry Velthuizen / Alamy Stock Photo; **p. 84** *bl* © Nick Hale/Getty Images, *t* © Roger-Viollet / TopFoto, *br* ©fazon1/iStock/ Thinkstock/Getty Images; **p.85** © ronniechua/iStock/Thinkstock/Getty Images; **p.86** © robynmac/ iStock/Thinkstock/Getty Images; **p.87** *l* © Yale Center for British Art, Paul Mellon Collection, *r* © AP/ Press Association Images, *b* © Fiona Hanson/PA Archive/Press Association Images; **p.88** ©ChepeNicoli/ iStock/Thinkstock/Getty Images; **p.89** *t* © Kenneth Garrett/Getty Images, *m* © Religious Images/ UIG/Getty Images, *b* © Eco Images/Getty Images; **p.92** *t* © Ray Stevenson/REX/Shutterstock, *b* © Myroslava Pavlyk/123RF.com; **p.93** © Pete Ryan/Getty Images; **p.95** © Martin Moxtr/Westend61/ Superstock; **p.98** © milosk/123RF.com; **p.99** *l* © SANCHAI LOONGROONG/123RF.com, *m* © Alex_533/ iStock/Thinkstock/Getty Images, *r* © Cristian Baitg/Getty Images; **p.102** © Yuri/iStock/Thinkstock/ Getty Images; **p.105** © robertharding/Alamy Stock Photo; **p.108** *t* © The Granger Collection/TopFoto, *b* © TMAX/Fotolia; **p.109** © Print Collector/Getty Images; **p.110** © Aidar Ayazbayev/Hemera/ Thinkstock/Getty Images; **p.112** © The Granger Collection/ TopFoto; **p.114** © Art Directors & TRIP/ Alamy Stock Photo; **p.115** *t* © Tjavarman3/iStock/Thinkstock/Getty Images, *b* © Muralinath/iStock/ Thinkstock/Getty Images; **p.116** *t* © Dinodia Photos/Alamy Stock Photo, *b* © rozmarina//iStock/ Thinkstock/Getty Images; **p.117** © ullsteinbild / TopFoto; **p.122** © DeAgostini/Getty Images; **p.128** © Spencer Platt/Getty Images; **p.129** © 1996 Clay Butler – Sidewalk Bubblegum; **p.131** Courtesy of the Library of Congress, LC-USF34- 009694-E; **p.132** © FREDERIC J. BROWN/AFP/Getty Images; **p.139** © Dan Bannister/Getty Images; **p.142** © Frederic Courbet/Getty Images.

t = top, *b* = bottom, *l* = left, *r* = right, *c* = centre

Text credits

Index